Unit B

The Inside Story

Cells and Body Systems

I WONDER

Science begins with wondering. What do you wonder about when you see pictures like these from inside a human body?

Work with a partner to make a list of questions you have about structure and function within organisms. Be ready to share your list with the rest of the class.

Heart muscle tissue
White blood cell

B3

I PLAN

You may have asked questions like these as you wondered about your body. Scientists also ask questions. Then they plan ways to find answers to their questions. Now you and your classmates can plan how you will investigate structure and function within organisms.

My Science Log

How are all organisms alike? How are they different?

What is the inside of my body like?

How do different body parts work together?

How can I protect myself from disease?

Microorganism

Collect sample

1. Neighborhood

2. ...from sch...

With Your Class

Plan how your class will use the activities and readings from the **I Investigate** part of this unit. Decide what other resources you might use.

On Your Own

There are many ways to learn about organisms. Following are some things you can do to explore the structure and function of organisms by yourself or with some classmates. Some explorations may take longer to do than others. Look over the suggestions and choose...

- **Places to Visit**
- **Projects to Do**
- **Books to Read**

PLACES TO VISIT

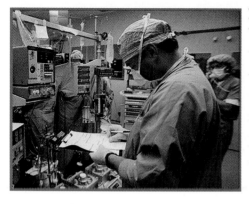

HOSPITAL

Arrange to visit a nearby health clinic or hospital. Ask for a guided tour of the medical and surgical departments, X-ray and other specialized equipment centers, and the lab. Be sure to ask about procedures for patients with highly contagious diseases.

CRIME LAB

In crime labs, experts analyze samples of hair, blood, and other body tissues to help the police identify criminals and victims. A community near you may have a regional crime-lab center. Arrange to visit the center and see the experts at work.

PHARMACY

Ask a pharmacist if you may observe as he or she fills prescriptions. Find out how different medicines are prepared. Ask about the uses of some of the medicines. If a pharmaceutical company is nearby, arrange for a tour to see how medicines are made.

WATER TREATMENT PLANT

At water treatment plants, water is analyzed for the presence of microorganisms that can cause diseases. Visit a water treatment plant near you. Find out how the water is treated to get rid of microorganisms.

PROJECTS TO DO

HEALTH VIDEO

Make a health video for younger students. Ask several classmates to help write a script or perform in the video. Your video should identify ways students can protect themselves and others from diseases caused by microorganisms.

SCIENCE FAIR PROJECT

Review the **I Wonder** questions you and your partner asked. One way to find answers to these questions is by doing a science fair project. Choose one of your questions. Plan a project that would help answer the question. Discuss your plan with your teacher. With his or her approval, begin work by collecting materials and resources. Then carry out your plan.

SYSTEM MODEL

Choose an organ or a system of the human body and make a model of it. For example, you might make a model of the lungs or of the digestive system. Use common materials, such as papier-mâché, modeling clay, paper-towel tubes, or lightweight cardboard, for your model.

MICROORGANISM HUNT

Collect samples of soil, leaves, and water. Be sure to ask permission before taking any samples from someone else's property. Examine your samples under a microscope. Look for microorganisms. Try to identify them. Sketch any microorganisms you see and tell where you found them.

The Princess in the Pigpen

by Jane Resh Thomas (Clarion, 1989). What a place to wake up— a pigpen on a farm in Iowa! That is just the first surprise for Elizabeth, who had been living in England in the year 1600. Join her as she learns about a different world, one with electricity, cars, sneakers, and, best of all, modern medicines. Read this book to find out whether Elizabeth can bring some medicines back to 1600 to save her mother's life.

AVON 0-380-71194-X
$3.50 U.S.
$4.50 CAN.

AVON CAMELOT

"A JOURNEY OF DISCOVERY AS MUCH FOR YOUNG READERS AS FOR THE TIME TRAVELER"
The New York Times Book Review

JANE RESH THOMAS
THE PRINCESS IN THE PIGPEN

Facing the Future: Choosing Health

by Alan Collinson (Steck-Vaughn, 1991). How do you have a healthy life? This book provides some answers. They include eating right, exercising, and not smoking. But the most important factor is living in a country with good medical resources. That's an important step to a long, healthy life.

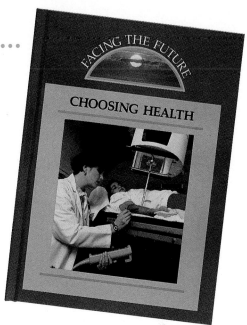

More Books to Read

Atoms and Cells

by Lionel Bender (Gloucester Press, 1990). In this book, you will learn about the microscope, how it works, and what it does. You will see pictures taken through a microscope, showing crystals and atoms. You will see chromosomes pictured 2,000 times larger than they really are so that we can see them. Imagine seeing the smallest parts of your-self 2,000 times larger than normal!

Could You Ever Live Forever?

by David Darling (Dillon Press, 1991). Do you want to live forever? That is a very long time, especially if you keep getting older and older. How would you look? This book will help you find out what happens as your body ages and what we have learned to help us live longer.

Native American Doctor: The Story of Susan LaFlesche Picotte

by Jeri Ferris (Carolrhoda, 1991). Read about Susan LaFlesche, who in 1889 became the first Native American woman to graduate from medical school. Her goal was to help her people, the Omahas. On their behalf, she worked all her life as an advisor and spokesperson to the U.S. government. Her dream was realized two years before her death when a hospital was built for them.

Outside and Inside You

by Sandra Markle (Bradbury Press, 1991). How does your body work? How do you grow and change? This book tells you about different parts of your body and what each part does. The photographs are amazing. Who would have thought we really look like that?

INVESTIGATE

To find answers to their questions, scientists do many things. They read, think, talk to others, and do experiments. Their investigations often lead to new questions.

In this unit you will have many chances to think and work like a scientist. How will you find answers to questions you asked?

▶ **COMPARING** When you compare objects or events, you look for what they have in common. You also look for differences between them.

▶ **CLASSIFYING/ORDERING** When you classify objects, you put them into groups according to how they are alike. Ordering is putting things in an order. For example, you might order things from first to last, smallest to largest, or lightest to heaviest.

▶ **INFERRING** Inferring is using what you have observed to explain what has happened. An observation is something you see or experience. An inference is an explanation of an observation, and it may be right or wrong.

Are you ready to begin?

SECTIONS

Cells

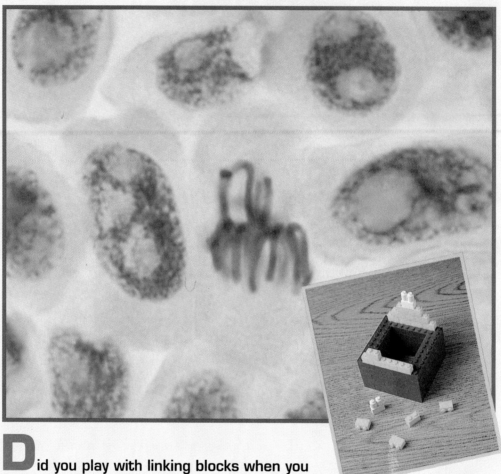

Did you play with linking blocks when you were younger? Maybe you built cars or skyscrapers with your blocks. You probably built many different things. Although they looked different, all of the things you built were made of the same types of blocks.

Now think about plants and animals. Each has many different parts. Yet the parts have the same basic building blocks. All living things on the Earth are made up of the same things—cells. In this section, you will take a closer look at these basic building blocks of living things. Keep careful notes in your Science Log as you work through some of the investigations in this section.

1 THROUGH THE LOOKING GLASS

For a long time, scientists did not have a way to look at very small things. The invention of the microscope changed that. The microscope helped scientists explore a world never before seen. In the activities that follow, you can use a microscope to discover what early scientists first saw inside living things.

ACTIVITY

Take a Closer Look

Do you like onions on your hamburgers? Whether you like onions or not, you probably have never seen inside one. In this activity, you will discover something new about an onion.

MATERIALS
- small piece of onion skin
- microscope slide
- red food coloring
- microscope
- Science Log data sheet

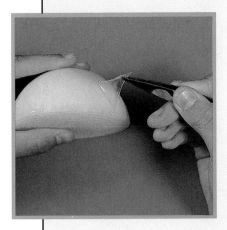

DO THIS

1 Break a piece of onion. Peel off a small piece of "skin," and put it on a microscope slide. Add a drop or two of red food coloring.

2 Place the slide under the microscope and adjust the focus.

3 Sketch what you see.

THINK AND WRITE

1. What did the onion skin look like under the microscope?

2. Do you think other parts of the onion would look the same? Explain.

What Does It Look Like?

Just as you did in the activity, scientists have used microscopes to make discoveries about living things. As you read, think about how exciting some of these discoveries must have been.

Working as a scientist in the 1600s, Robert Hooke spent many hours forming hypotheses, conducting experiments, and drawing conclusions. Yet he couldn't have known that doing something as simple as observing a piece of cork under a microscope would enable him to see something no scientist had ever seen before.

Suppose that you are with Hooke in his lab. He explains to you what he has done:

To Hooke the cork seemed to be divided like the sleeping rooms in a monastery. He decided to call them *cells*, which is what monks' rooms are called. The cork cells that Hooke saw looked very much like the onion you saw in the activity.

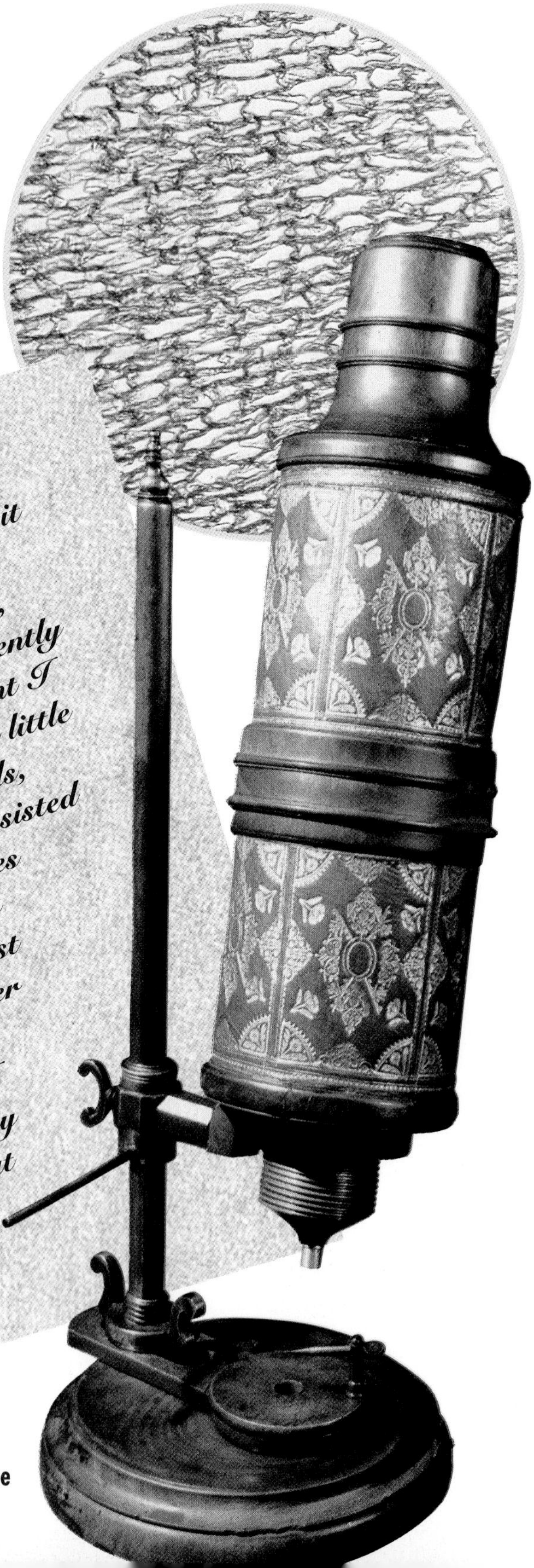

I took a good clear piece of cork, and with a penknife sharpened as keen as a razor, I cut a piece of it off and thereby left the surface of it exceedingly smooth. Then, examining the piece very diligently with a microscope, me thought I could perceive it to appear a little porous. These pores, or cells, were not very deep but consisted of a great many little boxes separated out of one long pore. These were the first microscopic pores I ever saw, and perhaps that were ever seen for I have not met with any writer or person that has made any mention of them before this.

▶ **Hooke's microscope**

Hooke's discovery of cork cells was just the beginning. Scientists wondered whether all living things are made of cells. For scientists it was like putting together the first few pieces of a jigsaw puzzle. But many other pieces were needed before the picture would be complete. For nearly 200 years, scientists continued looking for cells. Some looked at plants, while others studied animals. They shared their information and finally, in the mid-1800s, they had all the pieces they needed to finish the puzzle.

First, scientists discovered that all plants and animals are made up of cells. In fact, all living things—trees, people, dogs, mushrooms, bacteria, and amoebas—are made up of cells.

Second, scientists determined that the cell is the basic, or smallest, unit of structure and function in all living things.

Third, and this was the final piece of the cell puzzle, scientists found out that every cell can reproduce to form new cells. This completed cell puzzle is called the *cell theory.*

▶ All living things are made of cells.

QUICK CHECK

LESSON 1 REVIEW

❶ Why was Hooke's discovery of cells so important?

❷ In your own words, define the word cell.

B15

2 INSIDE A CELL

You have fingers, eyes, ears, and many other parts. Each part does something different. The same is true of cells. They have many parts, and each part does something different. Let's find out what the parts are and what they do.

Fantastic Journey

A good way to observe a cell would be to get inside to see what it looks like. It sounds impossible, but with virtual reality, a kind of interactive video, you *can* travel inside a cell. Put on your gloves and glasses; reach for the door. You are about to begin a fantastic journey through a cell.

As you open the door, you look around and see a glass-covered inner-space capsule. You step inside, find an empty seat, and buckle up as a guide seals the door. Your trip is about to begin.

Before you know it, a wave of water carries the capsule through the cell membrane. A *cell membrane* surrounds a cell in the same way that your skin covers your body. The cell membrane allows water, oxygen, and other materials to pass into and out of the cell.

As you enter the cell, something splatters against the capsule. "That's cytoplasm," the guide says. *"Cytoplasm* is the material between the cell's nucleus and the cell membrane." Inside the cytoplasm, you see many structures. But you are most interested in seeing the nucleus. You turn to the guide and ask, "Where is the nucleus?"

Your guide points it out and reminds you that the nucleus is the most important structure in the cell. "The *nucleus* is the cell's command center," she says. "It controls everything that goes on inside the cell."

Within the cytoplasm, you notice some things that look like red beans. You ask about them and learn that they are *mitochondria* (myt oh KAHN dree uh). "Mitochondria are like batteries; they provide the energy the cell needs for all of its functions."

You see many other structures that you can't identify yet. The guide calls them organelles (awr guh NELZ). An *organelle* is any cell structure that has a specific job to do. You've seen several organelles already. For example, the nucleus and mitochondria are organelles. You would like to see more, but your turn with the interactive video is over. You take off the gloves and glasses and decide to take another look at cells through a microscope.

THINK ABOUT IT

Why is the nucleus the most important organelle?

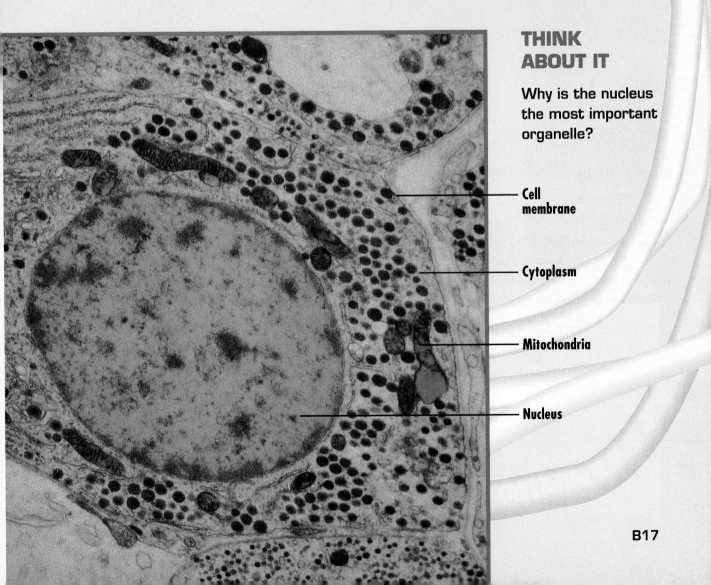

Cell membrane

Cytoplasm

Mitochondria

Nucleus

B17

ACTIVITY

How Are They Different?

You know that plants and animals are different, yet both are made of cells. Are their cells alike? In the following activity, you can observe plant and animal cells to find out for yourself.

DO THIS

1 Place a prepared slide of an animal cell under the microscope, and adjust the focus.

2 Sketch what you see. Label any organelles that you can identify.

3 Place a prepared slide of a plant cell under the microscope, and adjust the focus.

4 Sketch what you see. Label any organelles that you can identify.

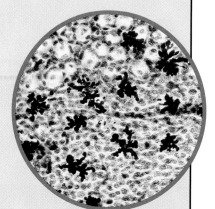

▲ Animal cells

THINK AND WRITE

1. What organelles did you see in the animal cell? in the plant cell?

2. **COMPARING** When you compare objects, you observe what they have in common and what differences they have. Carefully study your diagrams. How is the animal cell different from the plant cell? How is it the same?

Chloroplasts Plant cells are surrounded by a thick wall as well as by a cell membrane. A cell wall gives a plant cell strength and support. Plant cells also have many green organelles called *chloroplasts*. Chloroplasts are the sites of food production in green plants.

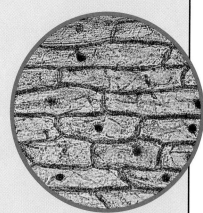

▲ Plant cells

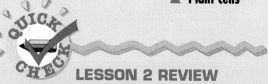

QUICK CHECK

LESSON 2 REVIEW

List all the organelles you have learned about so far, and write a short description of the function of each.

B18

3 IN AND OUT

On your fantastic journey, a wave of water carried your capsule through the cell membrane and into the cell. In this lesson, you will discover how materials really move in and out of cells.

Hot and Sweaty

It was a great game! Your team won the game, and you scored the winning point. As you head for the locker room, your friends are talking excitedly about the game. All you want is some nice, cool water to drink. You get thirsty when you exercise or when it's hot. Why?

▲ Your cells need water to avoid dehydration.

You're thirsty because you're sweating. Your body sweats to help keep you cool. Because you lose water when you sweat, you need to replace it. That's why you want that drink of water.

The cells in your body need water. If you don't replace the water you lose by sweating, you might become dehydrated. *Dehydration* means "loss of water." This happens when your body's cells lose more water than they take in. Dehydration can make you very sick. So go for it! Fill up those cells. Drink some cool, refreshing water, and enjoy your victory.

THINK ABOUT IT

Why do you think dehydration makes people sick?

ACTIVITY

Thirst Quencher

As you gulp water from the fountain, you wonder about those sports drinks you've seen advertised on TV. Do they really get into your body's cells faster than plain water? This activity will help you find out.

MATERIALS

- 2 jars with lids
- measuring cup
- water
- sports drink
- 2 hard-boiled eggs
- marker
- Science Log data sheet

DO THIS

1. Pour 300 mL of water into one jar. Into the other jar, pour 300 mL of a sports drink.

2. Shell the eggs, and place one egg in each jar.

3. Cover the jars. Use the marker to write the contents of each jar on the lid.

4. After 2 hours, remove the eggs from the jars. Measure the amount of liquid remaining in each jar.

THINK AND WRITE

1. Which egg absorbed the most liquid?

2. Do you think sports drinks get into your cells faster than water? Explain.

3. **INFERRING** Scientists often use what they have observed to explain what has happened. In this activity, you observed one egg absorbing more liquid than the other. What could you infer caused that to happen?

Movin', Movin', Movin'

Things are always moving in and out of cells. What causes all this movement? In this activity, you will observe one process that causes materials to move in and out of cells.

DO THIS

1. Fill the glass with water.

2. Put three drops of food coloring into the water.

3. Allow the glass to remain undisturbed for 15 minutes, and then observe.

THINK AND WRITE

1. What happened to the water?

2. Why do you think this happened?

Keep Those Cell Things Movin'

When you're hungry, you eat. When you're thirsty, you drink. Your body's cells need food and drink, too. In the last activity, you saw a process that causes things to move. Read to find out how this process helps move things in and out of cells.

Cells need water, nutrients, and other materials to do their work. They also need to get rid of wastes. One way materials move in and out of cells is through diffusion. *Diffusion* is the movement of material from an area that has a lot of the material to an area that has less of the material. In the last activity, you watched the diffusion of food coloring throughout the water. The food coloring moved from where there was a lot of it—the drops—to where there was less of it—the water.

Just as the food coloring spread, or diffused, throughout the water, materials diffuse into and throughout your cells. When your cells need oxygen, for example, oxygen outside the cells moves through the cell membranes and into the cells. When wastes build up inside cells, they move through the cell membranes to the outside of the cells.

Water is something your cells need a lot of. Remember, without water your cells become dehydrated. You help your cells get the water they need whenever you drink something. Water enters cells in a kind of diffusion known as *osmosis*. Osmosis is the diffusion of water across a cell membrane.

▲ **Diffusion**

Both plant cells and animal cells get the water they need through osmosis. You can see the effects of osmosis by looking at the plants in the photographs. The first picture shows

◀ The plant on the left is wilted; its cells are dehydrated.

▶ The plant on the right is not wilted; its cells are full of water.

a wilted plant. Its cells are dehydrated. When the plant is watered, water moves by osmosis from the soil into the cells of the plant's roots. From the roots, water travels in little tubes through the roots and stems to the leaves. In the leaves, water moves by osmosis from the tubes into cells throughout the leaves. The cells take in water and swell. What happens to the plant?

LESSON 3 REVIEW

❶ Why do you get thirsty when you exercise?

❷ Explain how waste materials, such as carbon dioxide, leave a cell.

❸ Is osmosis different from any other kind of diffusion? Explain.

4 MAKING COPIES

Have you ever used a photocopier? With it you can make an exact copy of something you wrote or an article you read and give it to a friend. Cells make copies of themselves, too. You can discover how they do this by reading and doing the activity.

ACTIVITY

Two for One

Remember the cell theory? According to one part of the theory, all cells come from other cells. In the following activity, you will see how this happens.

MATERIALS
- prepared slides of stages of cell division
- microscope
- Science Log data sheet

DO THIS

❶ Place slide 1 under the microscope, and adjust the focus. Draw and describe what you see.

❷ Repeat the procedure for slides 2, 3, and 4.

THINK AND WRITE

1. How were the cells you observed the same? How were they different?

2. What happens to a cell as it divides?

Chromosomes Within the nucleus of a cell are thin strands called *chromosomes*. Chromosomes contain the instructions that enable the nucleus to control all the activities of the cell. Before a cell divides, it makes an exact copy of its chromosomes. During cell division, the chromosomes and cytoplasm are divided so that each new cell receives a full set of chromosomes.

Cells, Cells, and More Cells

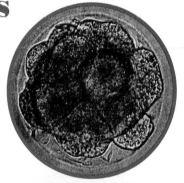

Close your eyes and slowly count to five, or look at a clock with a second hand and watch five seconds tick by. What happened? It's easy to think that nothing happened, but during those few seconds, your body made about 10 million new blood cells! That's right—10 million! Why do you need so many new cells?

What happens to your cells as you grow? Do they enlarge? Not much. As you grow, your body produces new cells. At the same time, many cells get old and die. Others wear away from the surface of your skin. Your body needs to produce more and more cells for growth and as replacements for old cells. New cells are produced through a division process called *mitosis* (my TOH sis).

Through mitosis, a cell makes an exact copy of its chromosomes, and then it divides. Where there was once one cell, there are now two. And two can quickly become four. Your body has several trillion cells, and most are able to make copies of themselves through mitosis.

THINK ABOUT IT

How does a cell "photocopy" itself?

▶ The trillions of cells in your body started from a single cell.

Let's Wrap It Up

Now that you've seen plant and animal cells and read about some important cell functions, let's summarize with a rap about the cell theory, written by a student in Cobb County, Georgia.

CELL THEORY RAP

by Deborah Carver

Listen close to the story I tell:
It's the rapping story of the living cell.
It's a happy tune that's sort of cheery,
About a real tough topic called cell theory.

All animals, plants, and protists too,
Are made of cells with different jobs to do.
They're the basic units of all organisms,
And I hope by now you've got the rhythm.

It all started with one dude named Hooke,
Who at some cork cells took a look.
He used a scope and took his time,
'Cause a cell is small and thinner than a dime.

Say 1, 2, 3, 4,
Are you ready to learn some more?
The animal cell has many parts,
And you must know each one by heart.

Like the farmer man in the dell,
The nucleus controls the cell.
It gives the orders—kind of like a brain,
And it's protected by a nuclear membrane.

Around the cell, you'll find another "skin."
This cellular membrane holds the whole cell in.
But its job isn't simple, there's no doubt,
It lets some particles go in and out.

Now please don't lose your science enthusiasm;
Listen to the story of the cytoplasm.
All around the cell this thick fluid does go,
But in the nucleus it will not flow.

And don't forget those ribosomes—
This is where proteins come from.
These protein factories are so small, you'll agree,
You need an electron microscope to see.

Just when you thought you weren't having any fun,
Along comes endoplasmic reticulum.
These tubelike structures serve as a track,
To carry stuff to the membrane and back.

Now have you ever seen doughnuts without any holes?
In a cell, they're called vacuoles.
They're filled with stuff like H_2O,
And they carry food so the cell can grow.

Last of all, but not the very least,
Mitochondria—mighty cellular beasts.
Since they turn sugars into energy so well,
We call them the powerhouses of the cell.

Now my friend, you know it well,
The unforgettable story of the living cell.

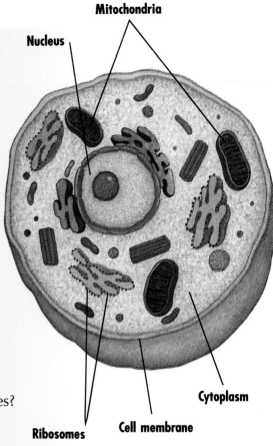

Mitochondria

Nucleus

Cytoplasm

Ribosomes

Cell membrane

LESSON 4 REVIEW

❶ What happens in the nucleus before a cell divides?

❷ Why is it important that your body has the ability to make new cells?

DOUBLE CHECK

SECTION A REVIEW

1. Why are cells considered the building blocks of living things?

2. How do materials move in and out of cells?

3. Why is it important that cells make exact copies of themselves?

SECTION B
We're Organized

▲ **Muscle cells**

Think about a bicycle for a moment. Bicycles have many different parts, and each part has its own job to do. You wouldn't get very far on a bicycle without wheels. And stopping a bicycle wouldn't be easy if it didn't have brakes. All the parts work together to make a bicycle fun to ride.

Like a bicycle, your body has many different parts. Each part has its own job to do. You already know that the basic units of structure and function in your body are its cells. And like bicycle parts, your body cells are organized into levels of structure and function.

In this section, you will discover how your cells are organized. As you complete the following investigations about body organization, keep careful notes in your Science Log.

1 FROM CELLS TO ORGANISMS

Look around your classroom. How many different living things do you see? Your classmates and teacher are living things. So are any plants or classroom pets you may have. Remember, all these living things are made up of cells. In the activities and readings that follow, you will discover how cells are organized to make up living things.

ACTIVITY

All Alone

Not all living things are as big as those you just counted. Some can be seen only with a microscope. In this activity, you will observe one very small living thing. As you look at it, think about how it is like you and how it is different from you.

DO THIS

❶ Place the prepared slide under the microscope and adjust the focus.

❷ Sketch the organism.

THINK AND WRITE

1. Describe the organism you observed.

2. How many cells did the organism have?

3. **CLASSIFYING/ORDERING**
   When you classify objects, you put them into groups according to how they are alike. How is this organism different from you?

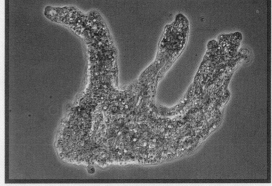

▲ Amoeba

Amoeba The living thing you examined is an amoeba (uh MEE buh). An *amoeba* is a single-celled living thing. Everything it must do to stay alive has to be done by its one and only cell. Like larger, many-celled living things, an amoeba moves, eats, and reproduces itself.

Muscle-Bound

You know your body is made up of many cells. But are all the cells alike? In this activity, you will look at muscle cells like those in your own body.

▲ Skeletal-muscle cells

▲ Smooth-muscle cells

▲ Cardiac-muscle cells

DO THIS

1 Look at the first slide under the microscope. Sketch what you see, and label your sketch *Skeletal-Muscle Cells*.

2 Look at the second slide under the microscope. Sketch what you see, and label your sketch *Smooth-Muscle Cells*.

3 Repeat the procedure for the third slide. Label this sketch *Heart-Muscle Cells*.

THINK AND WRITE

1. How are smooth-muscle cells and skeletal-muscle cells alike? How are they different?

2. Which types of muscle cells look most alike?

3. The muscles in your arm are skeletal muscles. Explain what that means.

Fantastic Journey: Part II

You've seen three different groups of muscle cells. What other cell groups are there? You can find the answer by taking another video tour. Put your virtual reality gloves and glasses back on, climb into the capsule, and buckle up. You're about to take another fantastic journey.

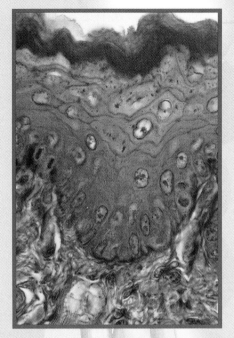

The first thing you come to is a vast field of cells. Cells are everywhere, as far as you can see. You finally figure out that you're looking at human skin cells—millions of them. Your tour guide reminds you that cells are the basic units of structure and function in a living thing. They're also the first of five levels of body organization. You ask your guide what the other levels are. She tells you that you will find out as you continue your journey. Just then your capsule plunges into a long, deep tunnel.

As your capsule clears the tunnel, you begin hovering above another group of cells. They look like the skeletal-muscle cells you observed under the microscope. Your guide asks what you notice about the cells. "They all look alike," you reply.

The guide agrees and continues: "They not only look alike, but they also do the same job. Groups of cells that have the same structure and do the same job are called *tissues*. Tissues are the second level of body organization."

▲ Skin cells
▼ Muscle tissue

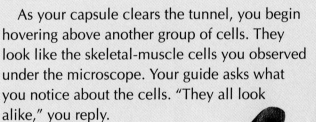

Without warning, the muscle tissue you're looking at seems to shorten and the capsule rocks violently! "Nothing to worry about," the guide explains. "This tissue is in the *biceps,* a muscle at the front of the arm. The owner of this muscle is just bending his arm. For that to happen, the tissue must contract. This shows one of the characteristics of tissues—the cells all work together." All the passengers in the capsule begin bending their arms and feeling their biceps.

The tour moves on. Soon the capsule begins rocking, as if to a musical beat. The beat gets louder and stronger. Now a throbbing structure comes into view. You know immediately where you are—the heart. You recognize the heart-muscle tissue. It's just like the tissue you observed in the activity. You also see tissues that don't look anything like muscle tissue.

Your guide explains that the heart is made up of several different kinds of tissues. "The heart is an organ that pumps blood throughout the body. An *organ* is a group of different kinds of tissues working together to do a specific job. Organs are the third level of body organization."

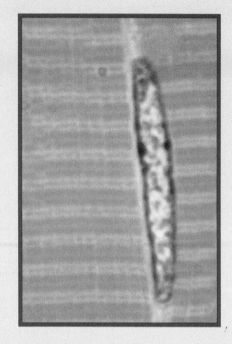

▲ **Muscle tissue—relaxed**

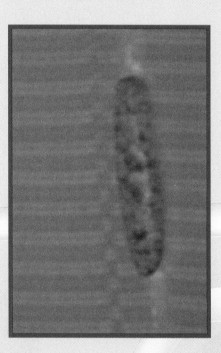

▲ **Muscle tissue—contracted**

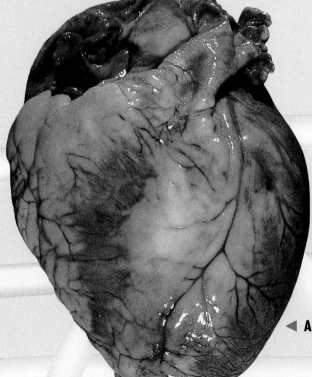

◄ **A human heart**

Before you have time to think about organs, your capsule races into a dark, windy passageway. "We're in a lung—part of the respiratory system," the guide yells over the howling wind. "A *system* is a group of organs working together to do a job. The respiratory system is responsible for breathing. Your body has several major systems. Systems are the fourth level of body organization."

Suddenly there is a loud noise like an explosion, and your capsule is hurtled into bright sunlight. "We must have irritated the owner's lungs, so he coughed us out," the guide explains. "I'm afraid this tour must end immediately."

You're back in your classroom. The video tour is over. But you haven't seen the final level of organization. What is the fifth level? Take a look in a mirror. *You* are an example of the final level. The fifth level of organization is the *organism*, a living thing that carries out all life functions.

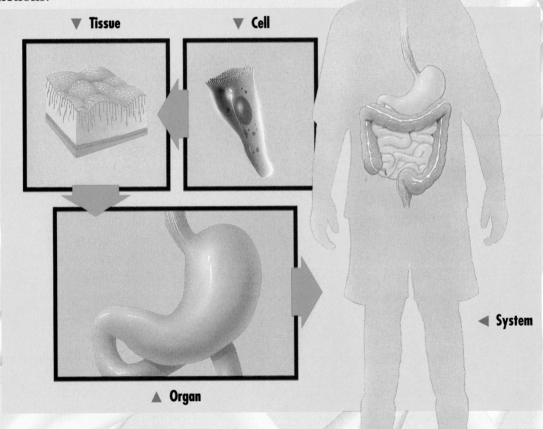

▼ **Tissue**　　　▼ **Cell**

▲ **Organ**

◀ **System**

THINK ABOUT IT

How are the five levels of body organization related?

What's That?

Through an imaginary video tour, you were able to see cells, tissues, organs, and systems. One photographer has developed another way to look at these structures. These pages show *his* fantastic voyage.

The Inside Story — A Fantastic Voyage Through the Human Body

by Beth Chayet from *3 2 1 Contact*

LITERATURE

Photographer Lennart Nilsson really knows how to get under your skin. His fantastic photos give close-up looks at the inside of the human body.

To photograph organs, tissues and cells, Nilsson uses a camera with lots of special lenses. To get an even closer look, he connects his camera to a scanning electron microscope. The microscope magnifies objects up to 100,000 times! The image appears on a TV screen, which Nilsson then photographs. The black and white photos are later colored by hand.

Nilsson works with scientists and doctors to get the inside scoop. He photographs body parts that have been preserved for research. Many of the cells are kept in laboratory dishes until he's ready to snap a photo.

Nilsson's photos give people a better understanding of how our body works. Here are just a few of his inside views.

Cleaning House

In each drop of blood are millions of red blood cells. They carry oxygen from the lungs to the rest of the body. After about 120 days, a red blood cell gets worn out and dies.

Magnified 10,000 times, this white blood cell is swallowing an old red blood cell. Luckily, every second, two million new ones are made deep in our bones.

Down Under

This underground cave is really the lining of the large intestine, magnified 400 times. About five feet long and two-and-a-half inches wide, it receives undigested food from the small intestine. The large intestine absorbs water from these pieces of food.

Food takes about 24 hours to pass through the body. It remains the longest in the large intestine, about 14 hours.

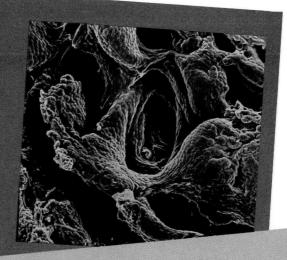

Go with the Flow

No yolk! These yellow globs, magnified 1,000 times, are fat droplets clinging to the wall of a coronary artery.

Arteries are blood vessels that carry blood from the heart to other parts of the body. Eating too many fatty foods can cause fat deposits to collect in arteries. This could block the arteries, causing heart problems.

The Whole Tooth

If you don't brush at night, here's what your toothbrush (the bristly stuff at top) has to remove in the morning: plaque. That's the invisible, sticky film that forms on your teeth. In 24 hours, bacteria living in plaque begin to eat away at the surface of teeth and cause cavities.

This tooth (magnified 75 times) was just pulled from a patient's mouth.

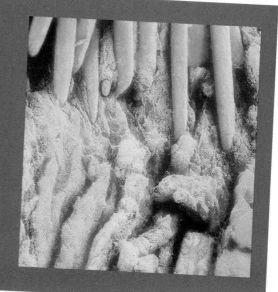

Say AHH!

Without them, food would have no taste. They are papillae (say: puh-PIL-ee), little bumps found all over the top of your tongue. They tell your brain when something is sweet, sour, salty or bitter.

More than 10,000 taste buds are in the skin around the base of papillae (here magnified eight times). Each taste bud has about 50 taste cells. They live about a week. But new cells always replace them.

Under Pressure

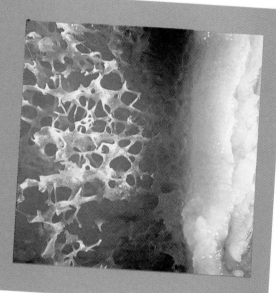

Sitting between the bones of the spine is a rubbery substance called cartilage. It acts as a shock absorber. It's also on the end of your nose and on the outer part of your ears. The sponge-like bone (left) and cartilage have been magnified five times.

Cartilage keeps these bones from grinding together. Otherwise, the bones would wear away!

THINK ABOUT IT

How can Nilsson's photographs help people better understand how their bodies work?

A Body of Riddles

Do you enjoy riddles? To summarize this lesson, you will use what you know about levels of organization to write riddles.

You will need: Science Log

Work in small groups. Brainstorm riddles about different levels of organization. Here's one to get you started.

> Riddle: *I am an organ of the human body. If I were a musical instrument, I would provide the beat. What am I?*
>
> Answer: *The heart.*

Try to think of a riddle for each level of organization. Write your best riddles and their answers in your Science Log. Also write the riddles, but not the answers, on a sheet of notebook paper.

Hold a Riddle Challenge by exchanging riddles with other groups and working in your own group to solve the riddles.

QUICK CHECK

LESSON 1 REVIEW

Do all organisms have the same levels of organization? Explain.

2 A SYSTEMATIC LOOK AT THE BODY

Every life function of your body is the job of a certain system. In the following activities and readings, you will examine one system in detail, and you will identify other body systems.

ACTIVITY

In Transport

In the United States, highways, railroads, and rivers provide ways to transport people and materials from one place to another. In your body, the transportation of materials from one place to another is the job of the circulatory (SUR kyoo luh tawr ee) system. In this activity, you will observe an important part of the circulatory system.

MATERIALS
- prepared slide of blood
- microscope
- Science Log data sheet

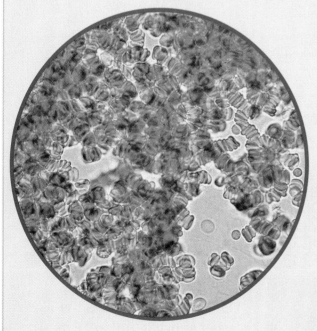

▲ Human blood

DO THIS

❶ Place the prepared slide under the microscope, and adjust the focus.

❷ Sketch what you see.

THINK AND WRITE

Describe the blood cells you observed.

Red-Blooded Tissues

If someone asked you to describe blood, you might say it's a red liquid. From your observations of blood in the last activity, you know that blood is more than that. Read on to find out just what blood is.

Blood is a fluid tissue that moves from place to place. It transports things your body needs, like food and oxygen. Blood is composed of two parts—a liquid part and a solid part.

The solid part of blood is mostly *red blood cells.* Red blood cells are like river barges. Their cargo is oxygen, and they carry it to body cells. The river is *plasma,* the liquid part of blood. Plasma is mostly water, but it contains nutrients and other materials, which it carries to body cells. Plasma also contains waste materials, such as carbon dioxide, which it carries away from body cells.

There are *white blood cells* in plasma, too. Although there are more red blood cells, white blood cells are huge in comparison. White blood cells help protect you from disease and infection. You will learn more about this later.

Plasma also contains *platelets,* which are pieces of white blood cells. These help form a clot to stop the flow of blood when you cut yourself.

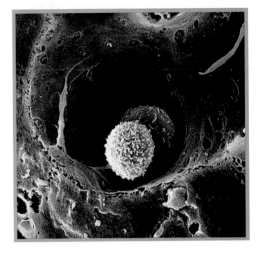

▲ White blood cell

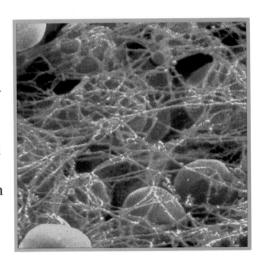

▲ Blood clot

THINK ABOUT IT

Why is blood a tissue?

▼ Red blood cells

Back in Circulation

You have learned that blood carries food and oxygen to your body cells. But how does it get around your body? You'll find the answer to that question as you do the following activity.

MATERIALS

- cooking baster
- tubing (40–50 cm)
- cup of water
- empty cup
- Science Log data sheet

DO THIS

1 Attach one end of the tubing to the baster.

2 Hold the bulb of the baster in one hand, and place the free end of the tubing in the cup of water.

3 Squeeze and then release the bulb to draw water into the baster.

4 Place the free end of the tubing in the empty cup. While holding the tubing, use your other hand to squeeze the bulb.

5 Repeat the procedure several times. Squeeze the bulb hard sometimes and not so hard other times. Record your observations.

THINK AND WRITE

1. What part of the circulatory system does the baster represent? What does the tubing represent? How does the water pulsing through the tubing feel to your fingertips?

2. Work with a partner to design another model to demonstrate how the heart and circulatory system work.

The Beat Goes On

In the last activity, you used a baster to pump water. The harder you squeezed the baster, the more water you pumped. In your body, your heart pumps blood. How does your heart increase the amount of blood it pumps? The following activity will help you find the answer.

MATERIALS

- stopwatch
- Science Log data sheet

DO THIS

1 Work with a partner. Find your partner's pulse by placing your index and middle fingers on the underside of his or her wrist. A person's pulse rate is the same as his or her heartbeat rate.

2 While sitting quietly at your desks, count the number of beats in your partner's pulse in 60 seconds. Record this number and label it *Heartbeat Rate at Rest*.

3 **CAUTION: Obtain your teacher's permission before doing step 3.** Have your partner run in place or do some other exercise for 1 minute. Once again, count the beats in your partner's pulse for 60 seconds. Record this number and label it *Heartbeat Rate After Exercising*.

4 Change places with your partner and repeat steps 1–3.

THINK AND WRITE

1. What was your partner's heartbeat rate before exercise? after exercise?

2. How is heartbeat rate related to the amount of blood the heart pumps in a minute?

3. **COMPARING** When you compare objects or events, you look for what they have in common. In this activity, you and your partner took each other's heartbeat rate. How did your heartbeat rate after exercise compare with your partner's?

Fantastic Journey:
Part III

You know that blood flows to all parts of your body, but exactly where does blood flow? Let's take another trip into virtual reality to find out. Gloves on, glasses on, buckle up—you know what to do.

This tour begins inside the heart. You're on the left side of the heart, and bright red blood cells are pouring into it. You ask, "Where is all the blood coming from?"

Your guide replies, "It's coming from the lungs, where it has just received lots of oxygen. That's why the blood looks so red. Oxygen is what makes red blood cells look blood-red."

Suddenly the floor opens up. Blood and your capsule drain into another part of the heart. You hear a low sound, sort of a "lub-dub," as the heart muscle contracts and you're pushed into a large tube. The guide calls this an artery. *"Arteries,"* she explains, "are thick-walled, flexible tubes that carry blood away from the heart. Smooth-muscle tissue in the walls of arteries helps control the flow of blood by expanding and contracting. Arteries carry blood to different parts of the body, but they can't pick up or drop off materials that cells need."

You wonder how cells get the materials they need. You get your answer almost immediately.

The movement of the blood is getting slower. You can see that the capsule is being pushed into smaller and smaller tubes. There is very little room between the capsule and the thin walls of the tube you're in now. You soon

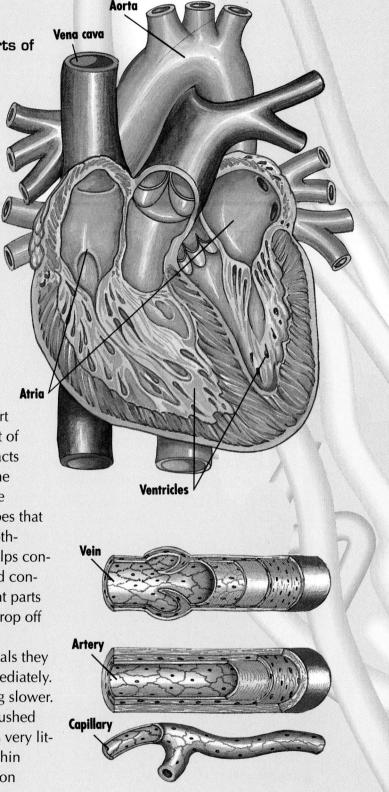

notice that red blood cells are flowing through the tube in single file. Your guide reports, "We are now in a capillary (KAP uh lair ee). A *capillary* is a very narrow blood vessel with thin walls. Capillaries are the smallest blood vessels, and they carry materials to and away from body cells. For example, oxygen carried by red blood cells diffuses through the walls of this capillary and into the surrounding cells. Cell wastes, such as carbon dioxide, diffuse through the walls and into the blood."

The red blood cells in front of you and behind you are now dark red. You ask about the color change, and the guide explains that it is due to the loss of oxygen. These blood cells have done their job and now must return to the heart. Your capsule will follow along.

You enter a series of larger and larger tubes and begin racing toward the heart. As you pass through each tube, a trapdoor closes behind you. Your guide announces, "We are now in the veins. *Veins* are blood vessels that carry blood back to the heart. The trapdoors, called *valves,* keep the blood from flowing in the wrong direction."

Your capsule now enters the right side of the heart. Once again, blood drains into another chamber and is pumped into an artery. This time, you are headed for the lungs. In the lungs, red blood cells drop off carbon dioxide and pick up oxygen. The cells turn bright red. You leave the lungs through veins and head back for the heart. You have now completed a round trip through the circulatory system.

THINK ABOUT IT

Describe how blood circulates through the body.

All Systems Go

You've had quite a ride through the circulatory system. But a visit to any of the body systems would have been exciting. Let's take a look at them all.

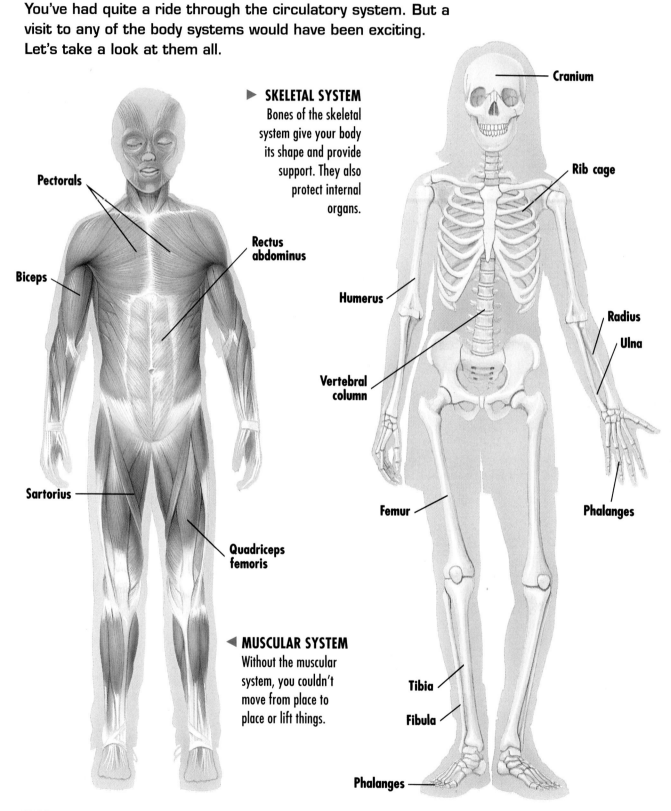

▶ **SKELETAL SYSTEM**
Bones of the skeletal system give your body its shape and provide support. They also protect internal organs.

Pectorals

Biceps

Rectus abdominus

Sartorius

Quadriceps femoris

◀ **MUSCULAR SYSTEM**
Without the muscular system, you couldn't move from place to place or lift things.

Cranium

Rib cage

Humerus

Radius

Ulna

Vertebral column

Femur

Phalanges

Tibia

Fibula

Phalanges

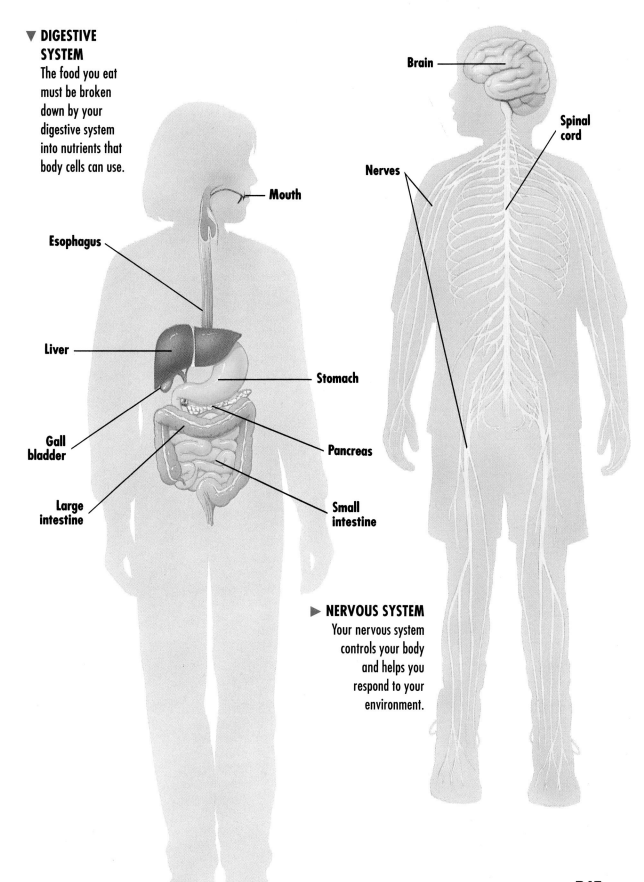

▼ DIGESTIVE SYSTEM
The food you eat must be broken down by your digestive system into nutrients that body cells can use.

Mouth

Esophagus

Liver

Gall bladder

Large intestine

Stomach

Pancreas

Small intestine

Brain

Spinal cord

Nerves

▶ NERVOUS SYSTEM
Your nervous system controls your body and helps you respond to your environment.

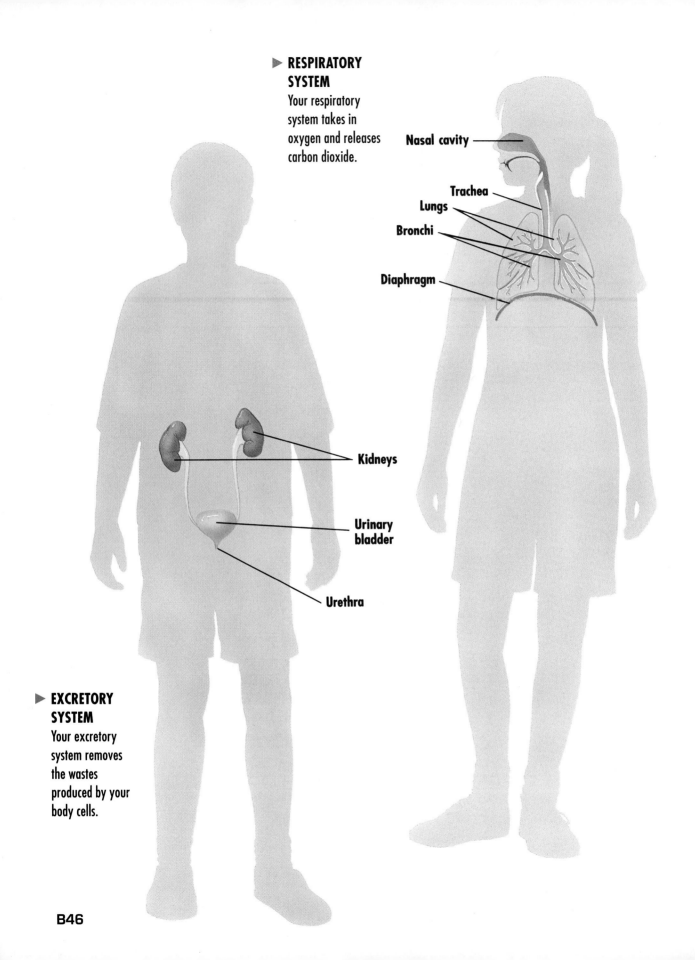

► RESPIRATORY SYSTEM

Your respiratory system takes in oxygen and releases carbon dioxide.

Nasal cavity

Trachea

Lungs

Bronchi

Diaphragm

Kidneys

Urinary bladder

Urethra

► EXCRETORY SYSTEM

Your excretory system removes the wastes produced by your body cells.

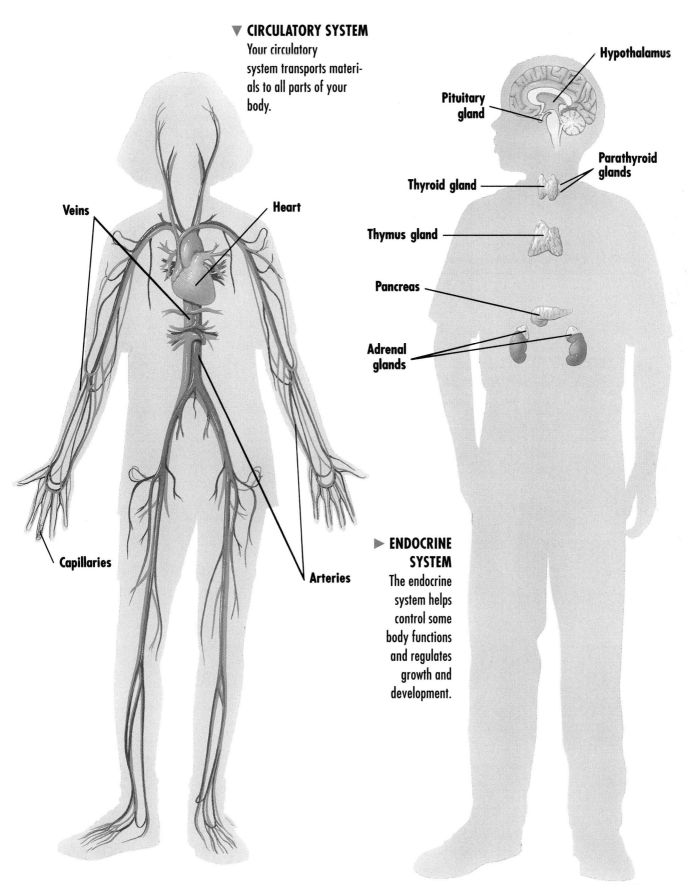

▼ CIRCULATORY SYSTEM
Your circulatory system transports materials to all parts of your body.

Veins

Heart

Capillaries

Arteries

Hypothalamus

Pituitary gland

Thyroid gland

Parathyroid glands

Thymus gland

Pancreas

Adrenal glands

▶ ENDOCRINE SYSTEM
The endocrine system helps control some body functions and regulates growth and development.

B47

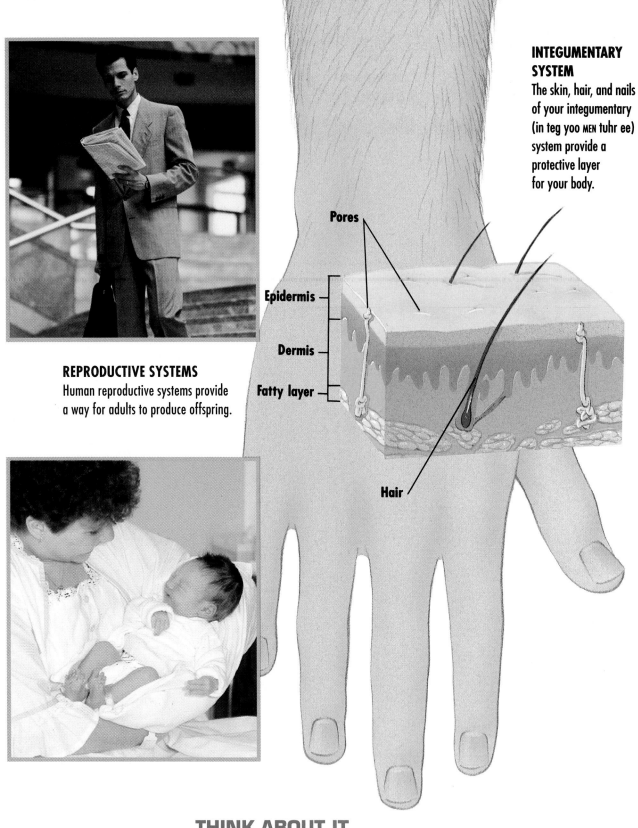

INTEGUMENTARY SYSTEM
The skin, hair, and nails of your integumentary (in teg yoo MEN tuhr ee) system provide a protective layer for your body.

Pores

Epidermis

Dermis

Fatty layer

Hair

REPRODUCTIVE SYSTEMS
Human reproductive systems provide a way for adults to produce offspring.

THINK ABOUT IT

Select one body system, and briefly describe its function.

All for One

You've seen that your body has ten systems, each with a specific job to do. Can one body system work without the help of the other systems?

You will need: Science Log

Try doing the following as fast as you can, and think about the body systems you are using.

- Smile.
- Close your right eye, and blink your left eye ten times.
- Touch your nose.
- Swallow.
- Breathe deeply.
- Close your left eye, and blink your right eye ten times.
- Clap your hands five times.

What systems did you use to do the first action, smiling? To smile, you needed your muscular and nervous systems. You used these systems and others to do the other actions.

The systems of your body work together. Every system depends on other systems to help it do its job. Your skeleton, for example, has joints so it can move. But it needs muscles to help it move and a brain to tell the muscles what to do. Your cells, tissues, organs, and systems form one working, magnificent organism—you!

LESSON 2 REVIEW

Describe a body activity and explain how it depends on the coordination of several organ systems.

DOUBLE CHECK

SECTION B REVIEW

1. Describe the different organs that make up the circulatory system, and tell what each organ does.
2. Give examples of the different levels of organization in one body system.

B49

In Sickness and in Health

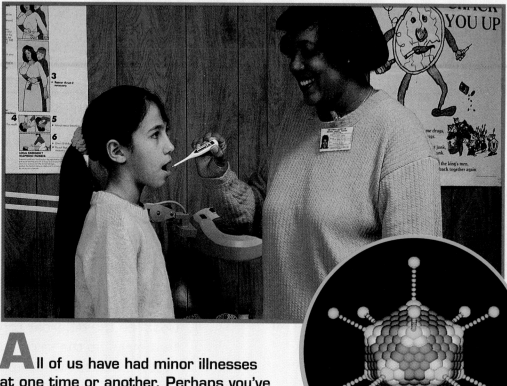

▲ Virus

All of us have had minor illnesses at one time or another. Perhaps you've recently had a cold or a sore throat. Maybe you had a fever. Most likely you were sick because tiny, disease-causing organisms entered your body and grew there.

What are these tiny organisms, and how do they get into your body? Once inside, how do they make you sick? How can your body protect you from them? The following investigations will help you answer these questions as well as others you may have about disease. Keep careful notes in your Science Log as you work through these investigations.

1 IT'S INFECTIOUS!

All around you are organisms so tiny that you can't see them without a microscope. Some of these tiny organisms, or *microorganisms,* cause diseases. In this lesson, you will find out how microorganisms enter your body and how they can be passed from one person to another. You will also discover one of the ways to tell if you have been infected by microorganisms.

ACTIVITY

Pass It On

You probably already know that many microorganisms can infect humans. Microorganisms cause everything from colds and flu to more serious diseases, such as chickenpox. In this activity, you can find out how some microorganisms travel from one person to another.

DO THIS

1 Tear one color of tissue paper into tiny pieces.

2 Place some of the pieces in your right hand. Shake hands with a classmate who has pieces of a different color in his or her hand. Repeat the handshaking with several other classmates. Note what happens to the colored pieces of paper.

THINK AND WRITE

1. How is the way the pieces of colored paper spread similar to the way microorganisms might spread?

2. In what other ways do you think microorganisms can spread?

On the Move

Your brother had a cold last week, and now you have one. Could he have given you the cold, and if so, how? Read the following story to find out.

from *Current Health*

"I feel terrible. My nose is running, my throat is scratchy, and my head hurts! Ah-ah-ah-ah-ah—chooo!" Ashley sneezed right into the phone.

On the other end of the line, her friend Bonnie jerked the phone away. "Don't make *me* sick, too!"

Ashley groaned, "I can't infect you, silly. You're not here!"

"Maybe not. But how did you get sick?"

Ashley glared at her brother. "It's Desmond's fault. I caught a cold from that little germ!"

Desmond hung his head. He felt ill, too. So did the rest of the family, and they all blamed him. "I'm not a germ!" Desmond pouted.

Just then his mom walked into the family room. "No, Desmond, you're not a germ. Ashley is just angry because she's going to miss her ski trip."

"He is a germ," Ashley whined. "He was the first to get sick, and then he passed it on to the rest of us. I learned all about it in health class. Germs are tiny living things called microorganisms. There are many

kinds of microorganisms in our world, but only a few kinds make us sick."

Desmond rolled his eyes. He thought he was going to get a boring talk on microorganisms. But then his mom told them something that made them both sit up. "A thousand microorganisms could fit in a line across the eraser of a pencil. There are trillions of them all around, even inside us, Desmond."

"Wow! What's a germ look like?" he asked.

"You," said Ashley, who was still angry.

Mrs. Layton said, "Don't be foolish, Ashley. You can't see microorganisms without a microscope. Some are round balls, some are twisted spirals, while others are straight rods. And under a very powerful microscope, you'd see many strange shapes. Some look like metal screws on top of spider legs."

Desmond tried to imagine tiny shapes swimming inside his body. "I don't see how rods or screws can make me sick."

"I do," said Ashley. "You need to know about the chain of infection."

THE CHAIN OF INFECTION

Mrs. Layton nodded. "In order for anyone to get sick, you need an agent. That would be someone or something that carries the microorganisms. Since you were the first to get sick, Desmond, you were probably the agent. Every once in a while the agent infects someone else. Then that person has the microorganism. He or she becomes an agent and gives it to someone else. It's almost like a game of tag."

Desmond asked, "You mean all you have to do is touch someone when you're sick and then she'll get sick, too?"

"Well, there's more to it than that," Ashley said. "There must have been an agent at your school. Maybe someone sneezed and didn't cover his mouth. You breathed the microorganisms into your lungs. Then you came home and took a sip of my juice. So I got the microorganisms. Then you wrestled your brother and coughed in his face. Then you fed the baby something with your unwashed hands and she got sick. Then you sneezed on the phone just before Dad got a call. That's how he got infected. See, it's all your fault."

Just then the phone rang. Ashley answered it with a big sneeze. Mrs. Layton gave Ashley a tissue. "Or maybe you gave the microorganisms to the others, Ashley."

Ashley grew very quiet. "I'm sorry, Desmond. Maybe you're not the only agent around here."

MODES OF TRANSMISSION

After the phone call, Ashley continued. "There are four ways that most microorganisms are passed from one person to another: by touch or physical contact, through the air, from food, and from insect or animal bites.

"The first, physical contact, is just like a game of tag. Microorganisms pass from one person to another—or from an object to a person. It can happen by sharing clothes or using the same fork or spoon. It can also happen when you cut yourself on something that's not clean. You get an infection.

"Microorganisms are also passed through the air. Like with a sneeze. By breathing in someone else's microorganisms, we can get a cold or the flu. Mr. Cullum, our health teacher, told us that in one sneeze there could be 20,000 microorganisms flying through the air. He also told us that sneezes could fly as far as 15 feet!"

Suddenly, Desmond understood. He smiled for the first time all day. "So if an animal is sick and it bites you, it sends the germs into your body!"

"Exactly," Mrs. Layton agreed.

Ashley yawned and remembered the ski trip. "And that's how you got us all sick, tick." 📖

THINK ABOUT IT

How are microorganisms passed from one person to another?

A C T I V I T Y

Hot! Hot! Hot!

MATERIALS
* graph paper
* skin-surface thermometer strip
* clock
* calculator (optional)
* Science Log data sheet

Mrs. Layton took Desmond's temperature and found that it was 38°C (100.5°F). Desmond had a *fever*, or a body temperature that is higher than normal. When disease-causing microorganisms invade your body, they may cause a fever. In this activity, you will find out what normal body temperature is.

DO THIS

❶ On graph paper, draw a horizontal line, and label it *Days*. Number the blocks along the line from 1 to 5. Draw a vertical line, and label it *Degrees Celsius*. Number the blocks along that line from 35°C (95°F) to 40°C (104°F).

❷ Place the thermometer strip on your forehead. Leave it there for 2 minutes.

❸ Have a classmate read the thermometer.

❹ Fill in the correct number of blocks to show your temperature for day 1.

❺ Repeat the procedure at the same time every day for four more days.

THINK AND WRITE

1. Study your graph. Describe any variations in your daily temperature.

2. Add the daily temperatures together. Divide the total by 5. You may use a calculator. This is an average of your normal temperature.

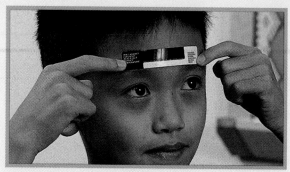

3. **CLASSIFYING/ORDERING**
Classifying is putting similar things in groups and ordering is putting things in an order. In this activity, you kept track of your temperature over several days. What was your highest temperature? lowest temperature? Arrange your temperatures in order.

QUICK CHECK

LESSON 1 REVIEW

❶ How would frequent washing of your hands reduce the spread of microorganisms?

❷ Describe several ways to stop disease-causing microorganisms from being passed from one person to another.

2 INVISIBLE INVADERS

Every day thousands of microorganisms invade your body. Some of them can make you sick. In this lesson, you will learn about several kinds of microorganisms and how they grow and reproduce on and inside the human body.

Fantastic Journey: Part IV

Several kinds of microorganisms cause diseases—bacteria, fungi, and protozoa. A virtual reality tour can help you find out what they are. Get ready once again to enter the microscopic world.

Your guide seals the capsule door tightly and announces over the intercom, "We're going to visit a world filled with disease-causing microorganisms. However, you have no need to worry, because the microorganisms can't penetrate our inner-space capsule. Ordinarily, microorganisms are so small that they can be seen only with a microscope. Here they're as big as our capsule. Hold on, we're approaching a *virus*."

You look out the window and see something that reminds you of a spaceship. You're told that this is a flu virus, one of several kinds going around this season. The guide points out viruses with different shapes—those that cause other diseases, such as colds, chickenpox, and polio. She also explains that viruses are very unusual.

◄ **Virus**

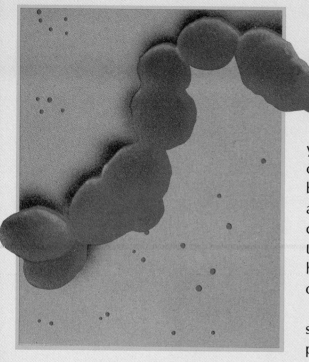

▲ **Bacteria**

▼ **Protozoa**

"We often think of viruses as microorganisms, but they really aren't. Remember, you discovered that all organisms are made up of cells. Viruses aren't made up of cells, so they can't be living organisms. They have none of the characteristics of cells—no membrane, nucleus, or cytoplasm. Viruses can reproduce, however, by taking over the cells of a host." You ask what a host is, and the guide explains that a *host* is an organism in or on which another organism lives.

Just then the capsule veers left, traveling next to something that looks like a huge chain of pop beads. "Take a good look," the guide says. "These are *bacteria*. Specifically, they're the bacteria that cause strep throat. Bacteria are true microorganisms. But the cells are very different from the ones you've seen before. For example, bacterial cells have no nucleus."

Suddenly, everything seems darker. A huge blob has plastered itself against the window of the capsule. You recognize the blob immediately and volunteer the information that it looks like the amoeba you saw with the microscope. "Right!" says the guide. "Amoebas belong to a group of microorganisms called *protozoa,* and some protozoa can make you sick."

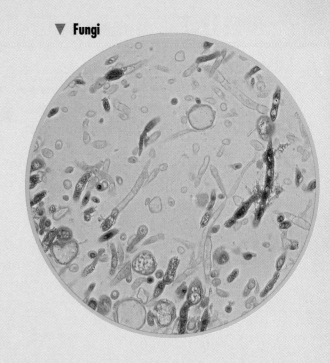

The capsule breaks the skin surface, races through a forest of hair covering a muscular leg, then dives into a valley with steep walls. The walls have deep cracks along their sides. "Where are we?" you ask.

"We're between someone's toes," the guide explains, "and this person has a bad case of athlete's foot. See those microorganisms over there? Those are the kind of *fungus* that causes athlete's foot."

"Wait a minute," you protest. "I read that the yeast my mom uses to make bread rise is a kind of fungus, but it doesn't cause disease."

"You're right," says the guide. "Not all microorganisms cause disease. In fact, most microorganisms, like yeast, are helpful."

Once again your tour has ended. You begin to think about all the different kinds of microorganisms you've seen. They seem to be everywhere.

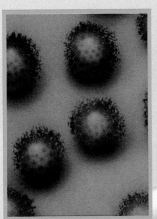 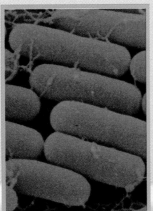  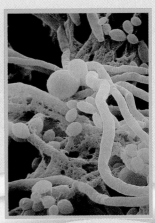

▲ From left: viruses, bacteria, protozoa, and fungi.

THINK ABOUT IT

What four kinds of microorganisms do these photographs show? What are the general characteristics of each?

"Rapid Grow"

Not only are microorganisms found almost everywhere, they also reproduce very quickly. One cell divides into two, two divide into four, four into eight, and so on. How many bacteria can be produced in one day? Try this to find out.

You will need: a calculator

Read each of the following situations. Then determine how many bacteria will be produced.

1. In warm conditions, bacterium A will reproduce every 10 minutes. At that rate, how many bacteria will there be at the end of 1 hour?

2. In cool conditions, bacterium B will reproduce every 90 minutes. At that rate, how many bacteria will there be at the end of 24 hours?

3. In very cold conditions, bacterium C will reproduce every 36 hours. At that rate, how many bacteria will there be at the end of 30 days?

Bacteria reproduce very rapidly, and they are found nearly everywhere on Earth. They live in hot springs and in snowbanks, in the air and in the ground. Most bacteria are harmless. In fact, many are used to make foods you enjoy. Did you know that yogurt is made with bacteria? But many bacteria, like the one that causes strep throat, are harmful. They make you feel sick by producing poisons, or *toxins.*

Remember, the bacteria that cause strep throat are round. Other bacteria may be shaped like spirals or rods. All bacteria have one of these three basic shapes.

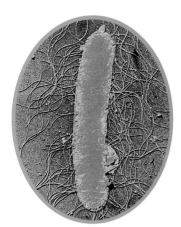 ▲ Rod-shaped bacterium

 ▲ Spiral-shaped bacterium

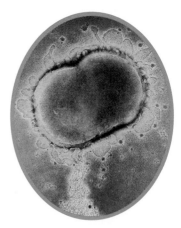 ▲ Round bacterium

ACTIVITY

Count Bacteria

Now that you know how quickly bacteria reproduce, imagine trying to count the number of bacteria in your classroom. How would you do it? The following activity will show you how to sample small areas and then to estimate, from those samples, the population of a larger area.

MATERIALS
* poster board
* marker
* ruler
* bag of dried beans
* calculator (optional)
* Science Log data sheet

DO THIS

1 Use the marker and ruler to divide the poster board into 12 equal-sized sections. Number each section. Then place the poster board on the floor.

2 Open the bag of beans and pour the beans onto the poster board. Allow the beans to fall freely.

3 Count the number of beans in section 1 of the poster board, and record the number.

4 Repeat step 3 for sections 6, 8, and 11 of the poster board.

5 Add together the numbers you recorded. Then divide the total by 4 and round to the nearest whole number. This is the average number of beans in the sections you sampled.

6 Multiply this number by 12 to estimate the total number of beans on the poster board.

THINK AND WRITE

How could this procedure be used to estimate the number of bacteria on a large area such as your body?

The Cold War

Bacteria reproduce rapidly but not as rapidly as viruses. Continue reading to find out how viruses reproduce and what diseases they cause.

On their own, viruses are about as lively as a rock. They can't eat, move, respond, or reproduce. But once they are inside cells, the story is very different. These tiny invaders completely take over cells, reproduce explosively, and make people very ill.

Recall that viruses are not organisms. They are nonliving pieces of hereditary material. The hereditary material is surrounded by a coat of protein. When a virus enters your body, it attaches itself to a cell and injects its hereditary material into the cell. The invaded cell can't tell the difference between its own hereditary material and the hereditary material of the virus, so the cell begins producing new viruses. Soon the cell has produced so many viruses that it can't hold any more. The cell bursts, and the new viruses look for other cells to invade.

Viruses cause many different illnesses. The colds that Desmond and his family had were due to a virus. Measles, mumps, and flu are also caused by viruses. All of these illnesses produce aching joints and muscles, headaches, and fevers.

THINK ABOUT IT

Describe the process of infection involved with "catching a cold."

▼ **Virus invading a host cell.**

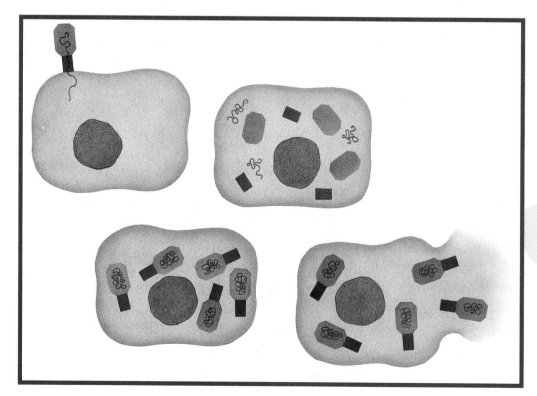

"I Think It's a Virus"

What other diseases are caused by viruses? The following list includes just a few of them. Try to find some others.

You will need: reference sources, Science Log

DISEASES CAUSED BY VIRUSES	
Cold sores	Rabies
Hepatitis	Polio
Mononucleosis	Yellow fever
Chickenpox	AIDS

Choose one of the diseases listed. Find out about the symptoms of the disease. If possible, find out what the virus that causes the disease looks like. Also, find out how the virus is spread. Luckily, not all viruses are spread as easily as the ones that cause colds. Finally, try to discover if there is a treatment or a way to protect yourself from the virus you choose. In your Science Log, write a short report about the disease you investigated. Share your findings with your classmates.

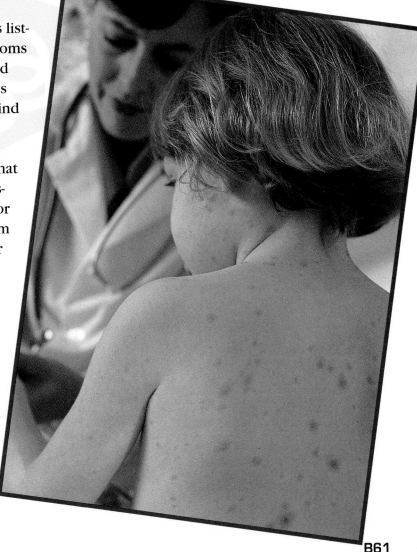

▶ Chickenpox is caused by a virus.

Parasites

Although bacteria and viruses cause most infections, some other microorganisms also cause diseases. Remember the amoeba you observed earlier? Amoebas belong to a group of microorganisms known as protozoa. Although most protozoa are helpful, a few can cause disease. Some fungi also cause diseases. Study these pages to find out more about protozoa and fungi.

◄ Protozoa live in moist places. Some live in damp soil or water environments like the one shown. A few protozoa are *parasites*—that is, they live in animals and plants.

► Unlike bacteria, most protozoa can move from place to place. An amoeba moves by extending part of its cytoplasm forward and then gliding into the extension. One type of amoeba can cause severe diarrhea if it infects the digestive system. This parasite may be found in contaminated food or water.

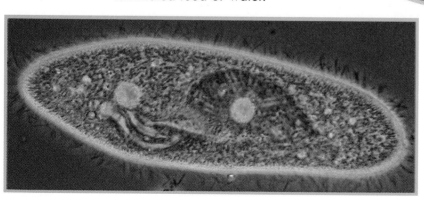

◄ Protozoa like this paramecium have hundreds of short hairlike structures that help them move through water. Most paramecia do not cause diseases.

▼ Although this protozoan cannot move on its own, it can cause malaria in humans. People become infected when they are bitten by a mosquito that is carrying the protozoan.

▶ The trypanosome moves by swishing a whiplike structure back and forth. This protozoan causes a disease known as African sleeping sickness, which attacks the nervous system. People are infected by the parasite when bitten by an infected tsetse fly.

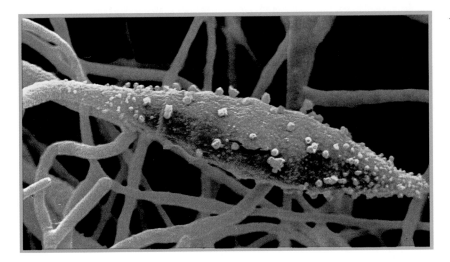

◀ Ringworm is one type of disease caused by fungi. Ringworm and athlete's foot are diseases of the skin. Some fungi attack the lungs or reproductive organs and cause diseases there. Fungi that cause diseases are parasites because they live off the living tissues of other organisms.

THINK ABOUT IT

Describe the effects of protozoa or fungi on the human body.

A Mystery to Solve

Although the microorganisms that cause most infections are well known, there are still mysteries to be solved. For example, Christopher seemed fine one minute and was violently ill the next. Read the following excerpt to find out what happened.

THE PUZZLE

by Elaine Landau from *Lyme Disease*

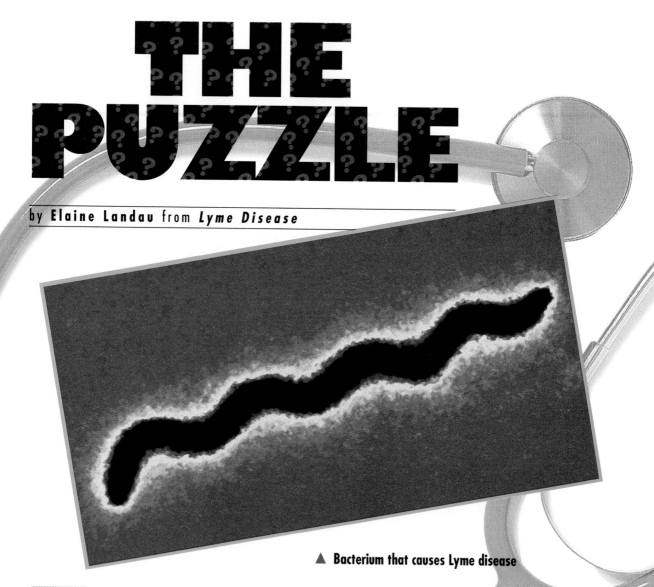

▲ Bacterium that causes Lyme disease

LITERATURE

It happened on a sizzling hot August day. Twelve-year-old Christopher stood on a swimming pool diving board in his northern New Jersey town. He paused before diving. Suddenly, a strong bolt of headache pain struck the left side of Christopher's head. It seemed to come from out of nowhere. The young boy later recalled how at one moment he'd felt fine, and

B64

then the next, his head throbbed with pain. Christopher broke out in a cold sweat. He felt nauseous and his body ached all over.

At first, Christopher's family and doctor thought he had a bad case of the flu. Yet something else was wrong. Time passed, but Christopher's symptoms remained. His doctor didn't understand why. He couldn't find any medical reason for Christopher's illness.

Christopher tried to continue leading a normal life. He attended school regularly. Christopher enjoyed sports and being out-doors, and he was determined not to give up any of his activities. But several months later, the situation worsened.

Christopher experienced an extremely sharp pain in his right knee. It happened while he was on a backpacking trip with his father and two brothers. The pain was so severe that Christopher could barely walk.

After returning home, Christopher's knee felt even worse. His parents took him to a number of doctors. Unfortunately, no one was able to pinpoint Christopher's baffling ailment. A bone specialist from a nearby city diagnosed Christopher's con-dition as an inflamed kneecap. The doctor prescribed aspirin for Christopher and had him begin physical therapy.

But nothing seemed to help. Christopher grew weaker, and eventually needed crutches to walk. He often felt tired and his muscles were sore. After a while, Christopher found it difficult to even carry his school books. By now, his right leg was partially paralyzed. At times, Christopher seemed to show improvement. Then, unfortunately, there would be relapses and he'd become extremely ill again.

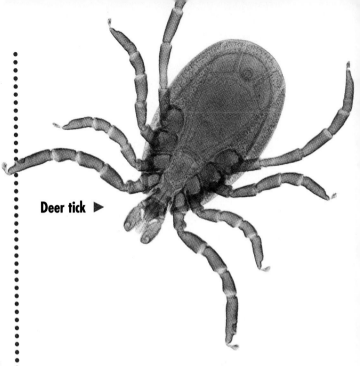

Deer tick ▶

Christopher's family continued to seek the help of different doctors. Finally, after another series of tests, Christopher was correctly diagnosed. Now he was given the proper medication. And after nearly eighteen months of suffering, Christopher's condition began to improve.

The strange illness that had struck Christopher and puzzled so many doctors was Lyme disease.

QUICK CHECK

LESSON 2 REVIEW

❶ Why aren't viruses considered microorganisms?

❷ How are protozoa and bacteria alike? How are they different?

❸ Why are some diseases, such as Lyme disease, so hard to diagnose?

3 ON DEFENSE

With so many disease-causing viruses, bacteria, fungi, and proto-zoa around, you might think that people wouldn't stand a chance of staying healthy. Fortunately, your body has ways of fighting these microorganisms. Medical science has also developed ways of treating infections and preventing them. In this lesson, you will discover the amazing defenses available to fight disease.

Fantastic Journey:
The Final Chapter

▲ Cilia lining the trachea

Your body is constantly working to prevent invasion by disease-causing microorganisms. A final virtual reality tour will give you a good opportunity to see just how this happens. Let's go!

 Once again your guide seals the capsule door as you adjust your seat belt. "Welcome aboard," she says. "Today we are going to see the human body defend itself against invaders. Our first stop is the respiratory system."

As you cruise down the throat and into the windpipe, or *trachea,* your guide asks you to look around carefully. "What do you see?" she asks.

"The walls of the trachea look wet and sort of shiny," you respond.

"Right," she replies. "The passages of the res-piratory system are coated with a sticky sub-stance called *mucus*. Mucus helps trap and kill microorganisms and other debris in the air that you breathe." The guide tells you to observe the tiny hairs that line the passages. "These tiny hairs also trap things, and they move in waves to 'sweep' foreign objects out of your body," she explains.

The capsule roars on through the respiratory system and into the bloodstream. Red blood cells are everywhere around you, but the guide asks you to look for white blood cells. "They're sometimes hard to find because there usually aren't very many of them," she says, "unless there is some sort of infection present."

Off in the distance, you see a giant cell coming toward you. "Look!" you shout. "There's one!"

Everyone looks as your guide explains, "White blood cells are the warriors of your body. These gigantic cells constantly move around, looking for disease-causing microorganisms. Whenever they find one, they swallow it whole!"

The capsule moves on to other parts of the bloodstream. Your guide tells you she is looking for antibodies. "What are antibodies?" you ask.

Your guide answers, *"Antibodies* are proteins that find and destroy specific kinds of microorganisms in the bloodstream." She goes on to explain that some antibodies occur naturally, while others are made when you receive a *vaccination.*

▼ **White blood cell attacking bacteria**

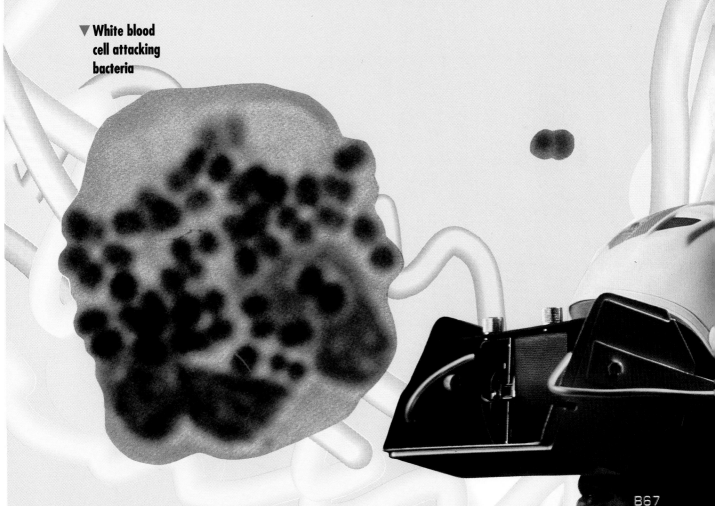

B67

"Antibodies have great 'memories,'" she says, "and some antibodies last a lifetime. For example, if you've ever had measles or received a measles vaccination, the measles antibodies are still moving through your bloodstream searching for any new measles viruses that may have gotten inside you. If they find any, they destroy them."

The inner-space capsule comes to a halt for the last time. It really has been a fantastic journey through the human body. After thinking for a minute, you ask your guide one final question. "Is it true that people probably wouldn't live as long if there weren't antibodies and white blood cells in their bodies?"

"Yes," she says, "as you've seen, the human body is a remarkable organism, but it needs to be protected. Take care of yourself," she calls out as you cross back into the real world.

THINK ABOUT IT

How does the human body protect itself from diseases?

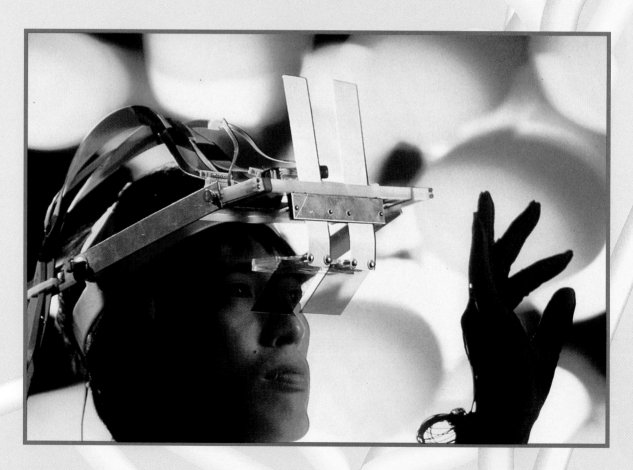

Lucky Shot

Scientists have developed many vaccinations to help your body fight invading microorganisms. Today, medical research is conducted under controlled conditions. In the late 1700s, however, that was not the case. Read on to find out how one doctor made a remarkable discovery about 200 years ago that led to the elimination of a dreaded and often fatal disease—smallpox.

In 1796, Edward Jenner, a doctor in Gloucestershire, England, risked his reputation—and the life of one of his patients—by performing a dangerous experiment.

Jenner made two small scratches on the arm of James Phipps, a healthy eight-year-old boy. Then Jenner took some pus from a cowpox sore on the hand of a local milkmaid and rubbed it into the scratches. Cowpox was a common disease that was easily passed from infected cows to humans. The boy soon developed a sore on his arm, just like the one on the milkmaid's hand. It was a minor infection, and it soon healed completely.

Six weeks later, Jenner took infected matter from a sore of a person with smallpox. At the time, smallpox was one of the most deadly human diseases known. Jenner rubbed the material into new scratches he had made on the boy's arm. The boy should have contracted smallpox in just a few days, but he didn't. Jenner had discovered a safe way of preventing a terrible disease—a vaccination that kept people safe from smallpox for the rest of their lives.

▲ Jenner vaccinating for smallpox

Since then, smallpox has been completely eliminated, and scientists have developed vaccinations against many other diseases. However, their methods are more scientific and don't risk people's health unnecessarily.

THINK ABOUT IT

In your own words, define *vaccination*.

ACTIVITY

Kills Germs on Contact

You could not possibly receive a vaccination against every kind of microorganism you might come in contact with. So another way to prevent infection is to kill microorganisms before they enter your body. In the following activity, you will discover a simple way to kill bacteria before they can cause infection.

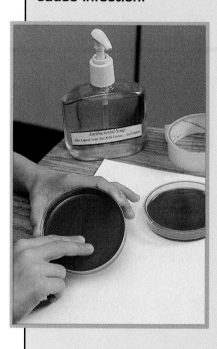

MATERIALS
* 2 disposable petri dishes of agar
* tape
* antiseptic hand soap
* Science Log data sheet

DO THIS

❶ Open one of the petri dishes, and gently rub your fingers over the surface of the agar. Close the lid and tape it shut. Write *Dish 1* on the tape with a pen.

❷ Wash your hands for a full minute with very warm water and antiseptic soap.

❸ Repeat step 1 with the other petri dish. Write *Dish 2* on the tape. Put both dishes in a warm, dark place for two days.

❹ **CAUTION: Do not open either of the dishes.** After two days, observe the agar surface of each dish. When you finish making your observations, give the dishes to your teacher for disposal.

THINK AND WRITE

Compare the surface of each dish, and explain any differences you observe.

Antiseptics As you saw in the activity, there are a lot of bacteria on your hands, and they need to be eliminated before they can make you sick. There are many things that can kill bacteria. Extreme heat and ultraviolet radiation from the sun work well but can't be used on your skin. Certain chemicals, called *antiseptics*, also kill bacteria. Many soaps now contain antiseptics. One of the best things you can do to prevent infection is to wash your hands many times a day with one of these soaps.

Helping Out

Antiseptics work well to kill microorganisms on the outside of your body, but they can't be used inside because they are too strong. There are, however, medicines that can be used to help fight infections inside your body. Read to find out how they work.

In the past, moldy meats, cheeses, and breads were used to treat infected wounds. Sometimes they worked, but nobody knew why. Then, in 1928, a British doctor, Sir Alexander Fleming, made a discovery. While trying to grow bacteria in a petri dish, Fleming noticed that some of his dishes were contaminated with fuzzy-looking molds. Many scientists had seen these molds, and they just threw their dishes away and started their experiments again. But not Fleming. He noticed that there weren't any bacteria in the areas where the mold was the thickest. He hypothesized that the mold produced something that kept bacteria from growing.

Fleming's hypothesis was right. The mold produced a chemical that prevented bacteria from growing. Fleming called this chemical *penicillin,* after the name of the mold. Penicillin was the first *antibiotic* discovered.

Since the accidental discovery of penicillin, scientists have developed many kinds of antibiotics, which have helped conquer most diseases caused by bacteria. However, antibiotics don't work against diseases caused by viruses because viruses aren't living organisms. They reproduce only in host cells.

One of the most serious diseases ever discovered—AIDS—is caused by a virus. The best hope for a cure for AIDS is to develop a vaccination to prevent it. But this may take many years. In the meantime, the best way to stop AIDS is to educate people on how to protect themselves from getting the virus. In the following article, you can read about a person who is leading the fight to stop this deadly disease.

Penicillin growing on petri dish ▶

THINK ABOUT IT

How are antiseptics and antibiotics different?

Dr. Helene Gayle:
Public Health Physician

Dr. Helene Gayle provides information to people about how to prevent disease. She is a public health physician who believes that the more people know about AIDS and how it spreads, the better they can protect themselves. Dr. Gayle wants people everywhere to know that AIDS can be prevented.

Dr. Gayle began her fight against AIDS while she was on the staff of the Centers for Disease Control in Atlanta, Georgia. The centers, known as the CDC, are part of the United States Public Health Service. The main function of the service is to prevent early death among the citizens of the United States. The CDC helps by finding ways to control or prevent diseases like AIDS.

Part of the work of the CDC involves learning how diseases spread. Dr. Gayle kept records of the numbers of people who had AIDS, where they lived, and what their lifestyles were like. Then she studied the data, looking for patterns that explained how the disease was spread and how the spread could be halted.

Gayle has left the CDC but not the fight against AIDS. She currently is chief of the AIDS division of the United States Agency for International Development. The agency has developed a program to improve health care in the developing countries of Africa, Asia, and Latin America, where AIDS is even more of a problem than it is in the United States.

Gayle's job with the agency is to provide health information and medical resources to assist in AIDS prevention. She believes that education is the best way to prevent the spread of AIDS. She wants young people to realize that lifestyle choices they make now may affect them their entire lives.

THINK ABOUT IT

Why is health information a good way to fight disease?

Medical Research

Vaccinations, antiseptics, and antibiotics are just a few of the ways modern medicine can help your body fight disease. They are usually a safe and dependable means of disease prevention and treatment. In this activity, you can learn more about modern medicine.

You will need: reference sources, Science Log

Use resources in your school or community library to find information about new vaccinations, antibiotics, antiseptics, or other ways to fight diseases. Find out about new ways to prevent or treat diseases such as AIDS, chickenpox, and flu. If possible, find specific information about new treatments, such as who developed them and when. How effective are they?

Write a short report in your Science Log. Then share your report with your classmates and discuss the importance of your findings.

LESSON 3 REVIEW

❶ How is receiving a measles vaccination similar to having the disease? How is it different?

❷ Why aren't antibiotics prescribed for colds and flu?

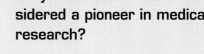 **DOUBLE CHECK**

SECTION C REVIEW

1. Why are infections caused by viruses more difficult to treat than those caused by bacteria?

2. Why are all disease-causing microorganisms considered to be parasites?

3. Why is Edward Jenner considered a pioneer in medical research?

REFLECT

It's time to think about the ideas you have discovered during your investigations. Think, too, about your many accomplishments.

SUMMARIZE

Answer the following questions in your Science Log.

1. What **I Wonder** questions have you answered in your investigations, and what new questions have you asked?

2. What have you discovered about the structure and function of the human body, and how have your ideas changed?

3. Did any of your discoveries surprise you? Explain.

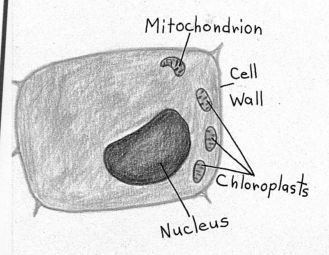

Plant Cell

Mitochondrion

Cell Wall

Chloroplasts

Nucleus

Plant cells have walls, but animal cells do not. Plant cells also have chloroplasts, which are organelles that produce food. Animal cells cannot produce their own food.

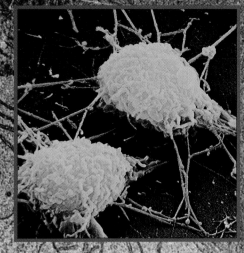

Animal Cell

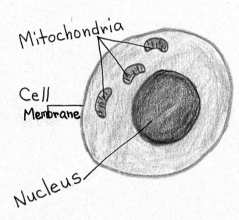

Mitochondria

Cell Membrane

Nucleus

CONNECT IDEAS

1. Describe mitosis as a part of the cell theory.

2. Give an example of a structure at each level of organization in humans.

3. Compare the usefulness of anti-septics for preventing infections caused by viruses and bacteria.

4. Describe several ways flu viruses can be passed from one person to another.

5. How does your body protect itself from disease-causing microorganisms carried by insects?

SCIENCE PORTFOLIO

❶ Complete your Science Experiences Record.

❷ Choose several samples of your best work from each section to include in your Science Portfolio.

❸ On A Guide to My Science Portfolio, tell why you chose each sample.

I SHARE

Scientists share their discoveries and ideas and learn from one another. How can you share what you've learned?

Decide

▶ what you want to say.

▶ what the best way is to get your message across.

Share

▶ what you did and why.

▶ what worked and what didn't work.

▶ what conclusions you have drawn.

▶ what else you'd like to find out.

Find Out

▶ what classmates liked about what you shared—and why.

▶ what questions your classmates have.

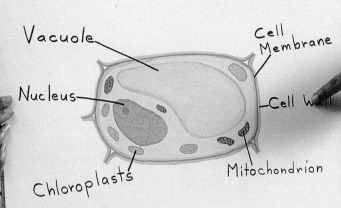

I ACT

Science is more than discoveries—it is also what you do with those discoveries. How might you use what you have learned about the structure and function of the human body?

► Set up a water stand for members of a sports team you belong to. You will need a jug of cold water, small paper cups, and a waste container.

► Call a sick friend, and ask if there is something you can do for him or her.

► Develop classroom guidelines for stopping the spread of colds.

THE LANGUAGE OF SCIENCE

The language of science helps people communicate clearly when they talk about the cells and the human body. Here are some vocabulary words you can use when you talk with friends, family, and others about human structures and functions and things that can affect them.

blood—fluid tissue that moves from place to place. It is made up of *red blood cells,* which carry oxygen to body cells; *plasma,* which is the liquid part of the blood; *white blood cells,* which help protect the body from disease and infection; and *platelets,* which stop the flow of blood at a cut. **(B39)**

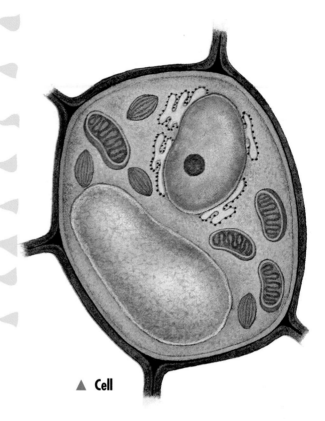

▲ **Cell**

antibiotics—chemicals that keep bacteria from growing. **(B71)**

antibodies—proteins in your body that destroy or weaken microorganisms. After you receive a measles vaccination, for example, your body produces antibodies that keep you from getting measles. **(B67)**

antiseptics—strong chemicals that kill bacteria. **(B70)**

cell—the basic unit of structure and function in an organism. In many-celled organisms, there are different kinds of cells, each with a different job to do. For example, muscle cells contract to produce movement, while red blood cells transport oxygen. **(B14)**

cell membrane—a protective covering around a cell. It allows certain materials to pass into and out of the cell. **(B16)**

cell theory—one of the major theories of life science. The cell theory has three parts: (1) All living things are made of cells. (2) The cell is the basic unit of structure and function of all living things. (3) All cells come from other cells. **(B15)**

chloroplasts—organelles that make food in plant cells. **(B18)**

chromosomes—structures in the nucleus of a cell that contain the instructions that enable the nucleus to control the activities of the cell. **(B24)**

cytoplasm—the living material between a cell's nucleus and its cell membrane. **(B17)**

dehydration—loss of water. **(B19)**

▲ **Diffusion**

diffusion—the movement of a material into an area that has less of the material. Food coloring spreading throughout a glass of water is an example of diffusion. **(B22)**

mitochondria—organelles that produce the energy a cell needs. **(B17)**

organ—a body structure made of different kinds of tissues that work together to do a specific job. The heart and the stomach are examples of organs. **(B32)**

▶ **Organ—stomach**

organelle—any cell structure that has a specific job to do. **(B17)**

organism—a living thing that carries out all life functions. **(B33)**

osmosis—the diffusion of water through a cell membrane. **(B22)**

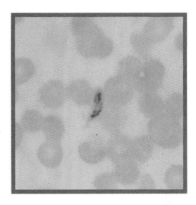

▲ **Parasite that causes malaria**

parasites—organisms that live by feeding on the living tissues of other organisms. The protozoan that causes malaria, for example, is a parasite that can live in mosquitoes and other animals. **(B62)**

system—a group of organs that work together to do a job. The human circulatory system, for example, is responsible for transporting nutrients and oxygen to body cells. **(B33)**

tissues—groups of cells with the same structure and function. The heart, for example, is made of heart-muscle tissue. **(B31)**

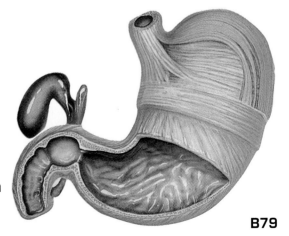

REFERENCE HANDBOOK

Safety in the Classroom

Doing activities in science can be fun, but you need to be sure you do them safely. It is up to you, your teacher, and your classmates to make your classroom a safe place for science activities.

Think about what causes most accidents in everyday life—being careless, not paying attention, and showing off. The same kinds of behavior cause accidents in the science classroom.

Here are some ways to make your classroom a safe place.

WATCH YOUR EYES.

Wear safety goggles anytime you are directed to do so. If you should ever get any substance in your eyes, tell your teacher right away.

THINK AHEAD.

Study the steps of the activity so you know what to expect. If you have any questions about the steps, ask your teacher to explain. Be sure you understand any safety symbols that are shown in the activity.

BE NEAT.

Keep your work area clean. If you have long hair, pull it back so it doesn't get in the way. If you have long sleeves, roll them or push them up to keep them away from your experiment.

OOPS!

If you should have an accident that causes a spill or breaks something, or if you get cut, tell your teacher right away.

YUCK!

Never eat or drink anything during a science activity unless you are told to do so by your teacher.

KEEP IT CLEAN.

Always clean up when you have finished your activity. Put everything away and wipe your work area. Last of all, wash your hands.

DON'T GET SHOCKED.

Sometimes you need to use electric appliances, such as lamps, in an activity. You always need to be careful around electricity. Be sure that electric cords are in a safe place where you can't trip over them. Don't ever pull a plug out of an outlet by pulling on the cord.

Safety Symbols

In some activities, you will see a symbol that stands for what you need to do to stay safe. Do what the symbol stands for.

 This is a general symbol that tells you to be careful. Reading the steps of the activity will tell you exactly what you need to do to be safe.

 You will need to protect your eyes if you see this symbol. Put on safety goggles and leave them on for the entire activity.

 This symbol tells you that you will be using something sharp in the activity. Be careful not to cut or poke yourself or others.

 This symbol tells you something hot will be used in the activity. Be careful not to get burned or to cause someone else to get burned.

 This symbol tells you to put on an apron to protect your clothing.

 Don't touch! This symbol tells you that you will need to touch something that is hot. Use a thermal mitt to protect your hand.

 This symbol tells you that you will be using electric equipment. Use proper safety procedures.

Using a Hand Lens

A hand lens magnifies objects, or makes them look larger than they are.

Sometimes objects are too small for you to see easily without some help. You might want to see details that you cannot see with your eyes alone. When this happens, you can use a hand lens.

To use a hand lens, first place the object you want to look at on a flat surface, such as a table. Next, hold the hand lens over the object. At first, the object may appear blurry, like the object in **A**. Move the hand lens toward or away from the object until the object comes into sharp focus, as shown in **B**.

▲ This object is not in focus.

▲ This object is focused clearly.

Making a Water-Drop Lens

There may be times when you want to use a hand lens but there isn't one around. If that happens, you can make a water-drop lens to help you in the same way a hand lens does. A water-drop lens is best used to make flat objects, such as pieces of paper and leaves, seem larger.

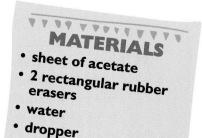

MATERIALS
- sheet of acetate
- 2 rectangular rubber erasers
- water
- dropper

DO THIS

1 Place the object to be magnified on a table between two identical erasers.

2 Place a sheet of acetate on top of the erasers so that the sheet of acetate is about 1 cm above the object.

3 Use the dropper to place one drop of water on the surface of the sheet over the object. Don't make the drop too large or it will make things look bent.

▶ A water-drop lens can magnify objects.

Caring For and Using a Microscope

A microscope, like a hand lens, magnifies objects. However, a microscope can increase the detail you see by increasing the number of times an object is magnified.

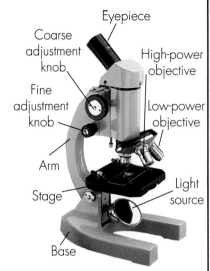

▲ **Light microscope**

CARING FOR A MICROSCOPE

- Always use two hands when you carry a microscope.
- Never touch any of the lenses of the microscope with your fingers.

USING A MICROSCOPE

1 Raise the eyepiece as far as you can using the coarse-adjustment knob. Place the slide you wish to view on the stage.

2 Always start by using the lowest power. The lowest-power lens is usually the shortest. Start with the lens in the lowest position it can go without touching the slide.

3 Look through the eyepiece and begin adjusting the eyepiece upward with the coarse-adjustment knob. When the slide is close to being in focus, use the fine-adjustment knob.

4 When you want to use the higher-power lens, first focus the slide under low power. Then, watching carefully to make sure that the lens will not hit the slide, turn the higher-power lens into place. Use only the fine-adjustment knob when looking through the higher-power lens.

Some of you may use a Brock microscope. This is a sturdy microscope that has only one lens.

1 Place the object to be viewed on the stage. Move the long tube, containing the lens, close to the stage.

2 Put your eye on the eyepiece, and begin raising the tube until the object comes into focus.

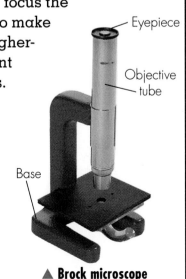

▲ **Brock microscope**

Using a Dropper

Use a dropper when you need to add small amounts of a liquid to another material.

A dropper has two main parts. One is a large empty part called a *bulb*. You hold the bulb and squeeze it to use the dropper. The other part of a dropper is long and narrow and is called a *tube*.

Droppers measure liquids one drop at a time. You might need to figure out how much liquid is in one drop. To do that, you can count the number of drops in 1 mL and divide. For example, if there are about 10 drops in 1 mL, you know that each drop is equal to about 0.1 mL. Follow the directions below to measure a liquid by using a dropper.

DO THIS

❶ Use a clean dropper for each liquid you measure.

❷ With the dropper out of the liquid, squeeze the bulb and keep it squeezed. Then dip the end of the tube into the liquid.

❸ Release the pressure on the bulb. As you do so, you will see the liquid enter the tube.

❹ Take the dropper from the liquid, and move it to the place you want to put the liquid. If you are putting the liquid into another liquid, do not let the dropper touch the surface of the second liquid.

❺ Gently squeeze the bulb until one drop comes out of the tube. Repeat slowly until you have measured out the right number of drops.

▲ **Using a dropper correctly**

▲ **Using a dropper incorrectly**

Measuring Liquids

Use a beaker, a measuring cup, or a graduated cylinder to measure liquids accurately.

Containers for measuring liquids are made of clear or translucent materials so that you can see the liquid inside them. On the outside of each of these measuring tools, you will see lines and numbers that make up a scale. On most of the containers used by scientists, the scale is in milliliters (mL).

DO THIS

1 Pour the liquid you want to measure into one of the measuring containers. Make sure your measuring container is on a flat, stable surface, with the measuring scale facing you.

2 Look at the liquid through the container. Move so that your eyes are even with the surface of the liquid in the container.

3 To read the volume of the liquid, find the scale line that is even with the top of the liquid. In narrow containers, the surface of the liquid may look curved. Take your reading at the lowest point of the curve.

4 Sometimes the surface of the liquid may not be exactly even with a line. In that case, you will need to estimate the volume of the liquid. Decide which line the liquid is closer to, and use that number.

▲ There are 32 mL of liquid in this graduated cylinder.

▲ There are 27 mL of liquid in this beaker.

Using a Thermometer

Determine temperature readings of the air and most liquids by using a thermometer with a standard scale.

Most thermometers are thin tubes of glass that are filled with a red or silver liquid. As the temperature goes up, the liquid in the tube rises. As the temperature goes down, the liquid sinks. The tube is marked with lines and numbers that provide a temperature scale in degrees. Scientists use the Celsius scale to measure temperature. A temperature reading of 27 degrees Celsius is written 27°C.

DO THIS

❶ Place the thermometer in the liquid whose temperature you want to record, but don't rest the bulb of the thermometer on the bottom or side of the container. If you are measuring the temperature of the air, make sure that the thermometer is not in direct sunlight or in line with a direct light source.

❷ Move so that your eyes are even with the liquid in the thermometer.

❸ If you are measuring a material that is not being heated or cooled, wait about two minutes for the reading to become stable. Find the scale line that meets the top of the liquid in the thermometer, and read the temperature.

❹ If the material you are measuring is being heated or cooled, you will not be able to wait before taking your measurements. Measure as quickly as you can.

▶ The temperature of this liquid is 27°C.

Making a Thermometer

If you don't have a thermometer, you can make a simple one easily. The simple thermometer won't give you an exact temperature reading, but you can use it to tell if the temperature is going up or going down.

DO THIS

1 Add colored water to the jar until it is nearly full.

2 Place the straw in the jar. Finish filling the jar with water, but leave about 1 cm of space at the top.

3 Lift the straw until 10 cm of it stick up out of the jar. Use the clay to seal the mouth of the jar.

4 Use the dropper to add colored water to the straw until the straw is at least half full.

5 On the straw, mark the level of the water. "S" stands for *start*.

6 To get an idea of how your thermometer works, place the jar in a bowl of ice. Wait several minutes, and then mark the new water level on the straw. This new water level should be marked C for *cold*.

7 Take the jar out of the bowl of ice, and let it return to room temperature. Next, place the jar in a bowl of warm water. Wait several minutes, and then mark the new water level on the straw. This level can be labeled W for *warm*.

MATERIALS
- small, narrow-mouthed jar
- colored water
- clear plastic straw
- ruler
- clay
- dropper
- pen, pencil, or marker
- bowl of ice
- bowl of warm water

— W

— S

— C

▶ You can use a thermometer like this to decide if the temperature of a liquid or the air is going up or down.

Using a Balance

Use a balance to measure an object's mass. Mass is the amount of matter an object has.

Most balances look like the one shown. They have two pans. In one pan, you place the object you want to measure. In the other pan, you place standard masses. Standard masses are objects that have a known mass. Grams are the units used to measure mass for most scientific activities.

DO THIS

❶ First, make certain the empty pans are balanced. They are in balance if the pointer is at the middle mark on the base. If the pointer is not at this mark, move the slider to the right or left. Your teacher will help if you cannot balance the pans.

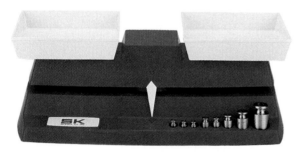

◀ **These pans are balanced and ready to be used to find the mass of an object.**

❷ Place the object you wish to measure in one pan. The pointer will move toward the pan without the object in it.

❸ Add the standard masses to the other pan. As you add masses, you should see the pointer begin to move. When the pointer is at the middle mark again, the pans are balanced.

❹ Add the numbers on the masses you used. The total is the mass of the object you measured.

▶ **These pans are unbalanced.**

Making a Balance

If you do not have a balance, you can make one. A balance requires only a few simple materials. You can use nonstandard masses such as paper clips or nickels. This type of balance is best for measuring small masses.

DO THIS

1 If the ruler has holes in it, tie the string through the center hole. If it does not have holes, tie the string around the middle of the ruler.

2 Tape the other end of the string to a table. Allow the ruler to hang down from the side of the table. Adjust the ruler so that it is level.

3 Unbend the end of each paper clip slightly. Push these ends through the paper cups as shown. Attach each cup to the ruler by using the paper clips.

4 Adjust the cups until the ruler is level again.

MATERIALS
- 1 sturdy plastic or wooden ruler
- string
- transparent tape
- 2 paper cups
- 2 large paper clips

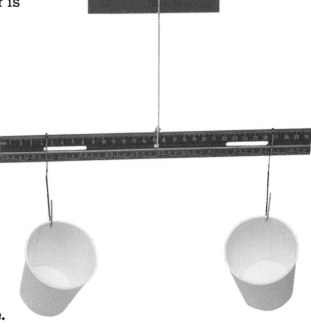

▶ **This balance is ready for use.**

Using a Spring Scale

A spring scale is a tool you use to measure the force of gravity on objects. You find the weight of the objects and use newtons as the unit of measurement for the force of gravity. You also use the spring scale and newtons to measure other forces.

A spring scale has two main parts. One part is a spring with a hook on the end. The hook is used to connect an object to the spring scale. The other part is a scale with numbers that tell you how many newtons of force are acting on the object.

DO THIS

With an Object at Rest

1 With the object resting on the table, hook the spring scale to it. Do not stretch the spring at this point.

2 Lift the scale and object with a smooth motion. Do not jerk them upward.

3 Wait until any motion in the spring comes to a stop. Then read the number of newtons from the scale.

With an Object in Motion

1 With the object resting on the table, hook the spring scale to it. Do not stretch the spring.

2 Pull the object smoothly across the table. Do not jerk the object. If you pull with a jerky motion, the spring scale will wiggle too much for you to get a good reading.

3 As you are pulling, read the number of newtons you are using to pull the object.

Making a Spring Scale

If you do not have a spring scale, you can make one by following the directions below.

▼▼▼ ▼▼ ▼▼▼▼▼ ▼ ▼▼
MATERIALS
• heavy cardboard (10cm x 30cm)
• large rubber band
• stapler
• marker
• large paper clip
• paper strip (about 1 cm x 3 cm)
• 100-g masses (about 1 N each)

DO THIS

1 Staple one end of the rubber band (the part with the sharp curve) to the middle of one end of the cardboard so that the rubber band hangs down the length of the cardboard. Color the loose end of the rubber band with a marker to make it easy to see.

2 Bend the paper clip so that it is slightly open and forms a hook. Hang the paper clip by its unopened end from the rubber band.

3 Put the narrow paper strip across the rubber band, and staple the strip to the cardboard. The rubber band and hook must be able to move easily.

4 While holding the cardboard upright, hang one 100-g mass from the hook. Allow the mass to come to rest, and mark the position of the bottom of the rubber band on the cardboard. Label this position on the cardboard 1 N. Add another 100-g mass for a total of 200 g.

5 Continue to add masses and mark the cardboard. Each 100-g mass adds a force of about 1 N.

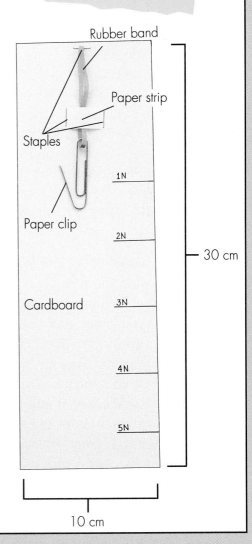

Rubber band

Paper strip

Staples

1 N

Paper clip

2 N

Cardboard   3 N

4 N

5 N

30 cm

10 cm

Working Like a Scientist

How Clean Is Clean?

In science class, Rachel and Rodney had learned about bacteria and how fast they multiply. They learned that some bacteria are helpful, that most are not harmful to people, and that some can cause diseases.

Rachel and Rodney had learned that disinfectants kill bacteria. They had also found out that there are many different kinds of disinfectants. Each type of disinfectant works a little differently. They wondered, "How can you know which disinfectant will work best for what you want it to do?"

Rachel and Rodney thought about this problem for a while. They put together what they already knew about disinfectants and then came up with a question that they wanted to answer. Rachel and Rodney asked, "Which type of disinfectant kills the most bacteria?"

DO THIS

Ask a question.

Form a hypothesis.

Design a test. Do the test.

Record what happened.

Draw a conclusion.

Often, solving a problem in science starts with reviewing what you already know and *asking a question* about something you want to know. When you review what you already know, you are putting together information and finding out where the gaps are in your knowledge. When you find out what you don't know, you can ask your question. In this case, Rachel and Rodney already knew some things about disinfectants, but they did not know what seemed most important—which disinfectant is most effective.

Rachel and Rodney knew that the next step in their investigation was to suggest an answer to the question. Rachel asked her father for four kinds of disinfectants. She explained that she wanted to find out how effective they are at killing germs. Her father let her look at the bottles but told her that he would send the disinfectants to the school, where Rachel and Rodney would be working on the investigation. Disinfectants are strong chemicals that must be handled with caution.

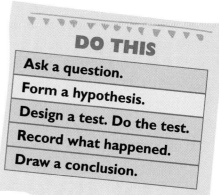

DO THIS

Ask a question.

Form a hypothesis.

Design a test. Do the test.

Record what happened.

Draw a conclusion.

Rachel looked at the labels on the bottles, but they all said similar kinds of things. One label claimed, "Kills any germ it touches." The ingredients in all of the bottles were different, and Rachel couldn't even read the names of most of them. She knew she couldn't figure out how each chemical worked.

Because Rachel did not know how the chemicals worked, she did not know which one would be most effective. She didn't see any reason why they all wouldn't work equally well. Rachel's suggested answer, or hypothesis, to her question was that all of the disinfectants would work equally well to kill bacteria.

The next day at school, Rachel shared her information with Rodney. He agreed with her reasoning, and they decided to use the four disinfectants Rachel's father had sent in.

When you use information to help you answer the question you asked, you are *forming a hypothesis.* A hypothesis is a possible answer to your question, or solution to your problem, that can be tested. Usually a hypothesis is tested by doing an experiment or by making a model. In some cases, the thing you are studying is so complex that you cannot really make a model of it or experiment on it, so you rely on careful recording of detailed observations.

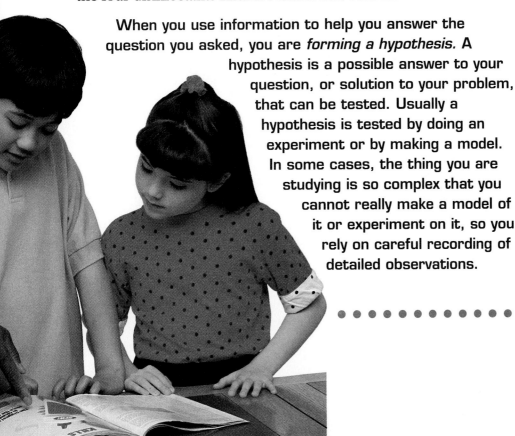

After you have asked a question and formed a hypothesis, you must somehow test the hypothesis. One of the most common types of test is an *experiment.* It is important to remember that a single experiment does not prove that a hypothesis is right. However, a single experiment may be enough to show that a hypothesis is not right and needs to be changed. The most important thing to remember when you are designing an experiment is that it must be focused on the question. For example, it is not useful to do an experiment that measures the pollutants in the air each day if you want to know how air pressure affects rainfall.

Rachel and Rodney worked with their teacher, Mr. Gormand, to design an experiment. They decided to grow bacteria in five dishes. Four of the dishes would be treated with different disinfectants. One of the dishes would be untreated.

Rachel and Rodney knew that it was important in any good experiment to have a control. A *control* is a sample or setup in which you don't change any variables. So the dish that was not treated with a disinfectant was their control. For any good experiment, you compare the results from your control to the results from your other samples to see if there is any difference. If there is no difference between the control and a sample, then the treatment you gave the sample had no effect.

Mr. Gormand showed Rachel and Rodney five dishes containing a substance that looked like beige gelatin. Mr. Gormand explained that the gelatinlike material was food for bacteria. He also explained that bacteria were added to the food substance before it was poured into the dishes. Then Mr. Gormand showed them four small disks made of absorbent paper. Each disk was soaked in a different disinfectant. Mr. Gormand placed a treated disk in each of four dishes. In the fifth dish, the control, Mr. Gormand placed an untreated paper disk. Mr. Gormand told Rachel and Rodney what to look for in each dish. As the bacteria multiply, they form colonies that are visible as little dots. As the bacteria increase in number, the colonies grow larger. Mr. Gormand told Rachel and Rodney that if a disinfectant killed the bacteria, a clear area— no colonies—would be found around the disk. The larger the clear area, the more effective the disinfectant. Each day, Rachel and Rodney would measure the width of the clear area from the edge of the dish to where the bacterial colonies started. They would measure the clear areas every day for five days.

Because it is very dangerous to work with live bacteria, Mr. Gormand did all of the treatments. He allowed Rachel and Rodney to handle the dishes only after the dishes were sealed, and he instructed them to wash their hands very carefully after recording their information for the day.

When you do an experiment, you must collect information. Another word for the information you collect is *data.* When you collect data, you are *recording your observations* and the results of your experiment so that someone else can understand what happened. You must not only record the information but also organize it. Organization is important if you want people to understand what you have discovered. There are many different ways to organize data. Two of the more common ways are making tables and making graphs.

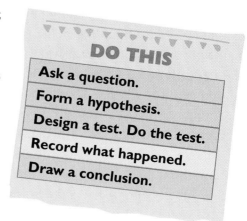

DO THIS

| Ask a question. |
| Form a hypothesis. |
| Design a test. Do the test. |
| Record what happened. |
| Draw a conclusion. |

Each day, Rachel and Rodney measured the clear area around each treated paper disk. They also observed the disk that was left untreated. Why did they need to look at the untreated disk? They recorded their measurements in a table each day. They then used the information in their table to make a line graph.

Often, information in a table is hard to read and understand. A graph is a good summary for many types of data.

Growth of Bacteria (Sample Data)

| | Size of Clear Areas (mm) | | | | |
	A	B	C	D	E (Control)
Day 1	20	25	25	30	0
Day 2	20	22	25	30	0
Day 3	19	20	25	30	0
Day 4	15	17	21	30	0
Day 5	10	15	15	30	0

Once all of your information is collected, you must use that information to *draw a conclusion.* One thing you are looking for when you draw a conclusion is to see if your hypothesis is supported. If your hypothesis is not supported by the results of the experiment, then it is most likely incorrect.

Remember, an incorrect hypothesis is not a failure! Not at all. An incorrect hypothesis helps you eliminate one possible answer to a question. You can then design experiments to focus on other possible answers. Also remember that if the experiment does support your hypothesis, that does not mean your hypothesis is proven. You may have to change your hypothesis a little as a result of your experiment.

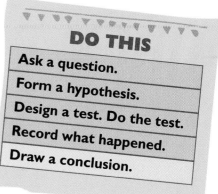

DO THIS

| Ask a question. |
| Form a hypothesis. |
| Design a test. Do the test. |
| Record what happened. |
| Draw a conclusion. |

You've already seen Rachel and Rodney's data. Look back at their hypothesis. Was their hypothesis supported by the data?

Rachel and Rodney concluded that their hypothesis was not supported. What they saw in the experiment clearly showed that some disinfectants worked far better than others. They concluded that the reason some disinfectants were better was that the chemicals in the disinfectants were different.

Rachel and Rodney still did not know how the chemicals killed the bacteria. And because each bottle had many different kinds of chemicals, they did not even know which of the chemicals was the disinfectant.

Rachel and Rodney concluded that they knew that disinfectants differed in their ability to control bacteria, but they did not know why this was so. Rachel suggested that they might continue their experiments by testing two very similar disinfectants. They could compare the actions of the two mixtures and then decide what contributed most to the disinfectant.

Often conclusions in experiments will raise other questions for which you might want to find answers. The solutions to problems often raise new problems to solve. This is one way in which progress is made in science.

INDEX

Note: Page numbers in italics indicate illustrations.

ACKNOWLEDGMENTS

For permission to reprint copyrighted material, grateful acknowledgment is made to the following sources:

Career World® Magazine: "So, You Wanna Be a Chef? Be Prepared . . . to Train Like an Athlete" by Joanne Koch from *Career World®* Magazine, May 1992. Text copyright © 1992 by Weekly Reader Corporation. Published by Weekly Reader Corporation.

Carolrhoda Books, Inc., Minneapolis, MN: Cover photograph by Cheryl Walsh Bellville from *American Bison* by Ruth Berman. Photograph copyright © 1992 by Cheryl Walsh Bellville. Cover illustration by Peter J. Thornton from *Everybody Cooks Rice* by Norah Dooley. Copyright © 1991 by Carolrhoda Books, Inc.

Children's Television Workshop, New York, NY: "The Inside Story: A Fantastic Voyage Through the Human Body" by Beth Chayet from *3-2-1 Contact* Magazine, June 1992. Text copyright 1992 by Children's Television Workshop. "Incredible Edibles: Unusual Food from Around the World" by Elizabeth Keyishian from *3-2-1 Contact* Magazine, June 1989. Text copyright 1989 by Children's Television Workshop. "Do Me a Flavor! Scientists Cook Up New Tastes" by Eric Weiner from *3-2-1 Contact* Magazine, May 1989. Text copyright 1989 by Children's Television Workshop.

Clarion Books, a Houghton Mifflin Company imprint: Cover illustration by Alix Berenzy from *The Princess in the Pigpen* by Jane Resh Thomas. Illustration © 1989 by Alix Berenzy.

Crown Publishers, Inc.: Cover photograph from *Voyager: An Adventure to the Edge of the Solar System* by Sally Ride and Tam O'Shaughnessy. Photograph © 1991 by Roger Ressmeyer/Starlight.

Current Health 1® Magazine: "Food Additives: A Closer Look at Labels" from *Current Health 1®* Magazine, February 1989. Text copyright © 1989 by Weekly Reader Corporation. "Preserving the Prairie—A Return to Tallgrass" from *Current Health 1®* Magazine, December 1993. Text copyright © 1993 by Weekly Reader Corporation. From "Stop That Germ!" in *Current Health 1®* Magazine, October 1993. Text copyright © 1993 by Weekly Reader Corporation. *Current Health 1®* Magazine is published by Weekly Reader Corporation.

Delacorte Press, a division of Bantam Doubleday Dell Publishing Group, Inc.: Cover illustration by Neal McPheeters from *Wings: The Last Book of the Bromeliad* by Terry Pratchett. Illustration copyright © 1991 by Neal McPheeters.

Dorling Kindersley, Inc.: Cover illustration from *Weather* by John Farndon. Copyright © 1992 by Dorling Kindersley Ltd., London.

Aileen Fisher: "Clouds" by Aileen Fisher from *In the Woods, in the Meadow, in the Sky.* Text copyright © 1965 by Scribner's, New York.

David R. Godine, Publisher, Inc.: Cover illustration by Jonathan Allen from *Burton & Stanley* by Frank O'Rourke. Illustration copyright © 1993 by Jonathan Allen.

Greenwillow Books, a division of William Morrow & Company, Inc.: "No, I Won't Turn Orange" from *The New Kid on the Block* by Jack Prelutsky. Text copyright © 1984 by Jack Prelutsky.

Peggy Guthart: "Ready for Spaghetti" by Peggy Guthart. Text copyright 1991 by Peggy Guthart.

Holt, Rinehart and Winston, Inc.: From "David Powless, Conservationist" in *Holt Life Science.* Text copyright © 1994 by Holt, Rinehart and Winston, Inc.

Dean Kennedy: Cover illustration by Dean Kennedy from *Burton's Zoom Zoom Va-ROOM Machine* by Dorothy Haas. Illustration copyright © 1990 by Dean Kennedy.

Alfred A. Knopf, Inc.: "January" from *A Child's Calendar* by John Updike. Text copyright © 1965 by John Updike; text copyright renewed 1993 by John Updike.

Lodestar Books, an affiliate of Dutton Children's Books, a division of Penguin Books USA Inc.: Cover illustration by Ted Enik from *Why Can't You Unscramble an Egg?* by Vicki Cobb. Illustration copyright © 1990 by Ted Enik.

The Millbrook Press: Cover illustration by Sal Murdocca from *EUREKA! It's an Automobile!* by Jeanne Bendick. Illustration copyright © 1992 by Sal Murdocca.

National Geographic WORLD: "The Great Flood of 1993" by Barbara Brownell from *National Geographic WORLD* Magazine, October 1993. Text copyright 1993 by National Geographic Society. "Surviving Andrew, 1992's Biggest Hurricane" by Judith E. Rinard from *National Geographic WORLD* Magazine, April 1993. Text copyright 1993 by National Geographic Society. From "Seeing Stars" by Judith E. Rinard in *National Geographic WORLD* Magazine, July 1993. Text copyright 1993 by National Geographic Society. "Chute for the (Sports) Stars" from *National Geographic WORLD* Magazine, July 1993. Text copyright 1993 by National Geographic Society.

National Wildlife Federation: "I Spy on Prairie Dogs" by Mark Hoogland, as told to Gary Turbak from *Ranger Rick* Magazine, September 1988. Text copyright 1988 by the National Wildlife Federation. "Lightning" by Robert Irby from *Ranger Rick* Magazine, August 1983. Text copyright 1983 by the National Wildlife Federation.

William Noonan: Cover illustration by William Noonan from *The Place of Lions* by Eric Campbell. Copyright © 1991, 1990 by Eric Campbell. Published by Harcourt Brace & Company.

Scholastic Inc.: "Cell Theory Rap" by Deborah Carver from *SCIENCE WORLD,* October 1990. Text copyright © 1990 by Scholastic Inc.

Steck-Vaughn Company: Cover design from *Facing the Future: Choosing Health* by Alan Collinson.

University of Nebraska Press: From p. 95 in *Dust Bowl Diary* by Ann Marie Low. Text copyright 1984 by the University of Nebraska Press.

Franklin Watts, Inc., New York: From *Lyme Disease* (Retitled: "The Puzzle") by Elaine Landau. Text copyright © 1990 by Elaine Landau.

PHOTOGRAPHY CREDITS:
KEY: (t)top, (b)bottom, (l)left, (r)right, (c)center, (bg)background

FRONT COVER, Harcourt Brace & Co. Photographs: (tl), (tr), (b), Greg Leary. **All Other Photographs:** (c), Terje Rakke/The Image Bank; (cr), Ewing Galloway.

BACK COVER, (tl), Biophoto Assoc./Science Source/Photo Researchers; (tr), Phil Degginger/Bruce Coleman, Inc.; (b), Antony Miles/Bruce Coleman, Inc.

TABLE OF CONTENTS, Harcourt Brace & Co. Photographs: Page:iv(br), Terry D. Sinclair; vii(tr), Weronica Ankarorn; vii(br), Terry D. Sinclair; viii(b), Terry D. Sinclair; ix(tl), Weronica Ankarorn.

All Other Photographs: Page: iv(tl), Photri; iv(tr), Runk/Schoenberger/Grant Heilman; iv(bl), Peter Menzel; v(tr), David A. Wagner/PHOTOTAKE; v(bl), NIBSC/SPL/Photo Researchers; v(br), Peter Menzel; vi(tl), Roger Ressmeyer/Starlight; vi(tr), Giraudon/Art Resource; vi(b), NASA/JSC/Starlight; vii(tl), David R. Frazier Photolibrary; vii(bl), First Light; viii(tl), L.L. Rue, Jr./Bruce Coleman, Inc.; viii(tr), Amy Etra/PhotoEdit; viii-ix(b), Lefever/Grushow/Grant Heilman Photography; ix(tr), Ann Purcell/Photo Researchers; ix(br), Mike Khansa/The Image Bank.

TO THE STUDENT: Harcourt Brace & Company Photographs: Page:xi(b), xiii, xvi(l), Terry D. Sinclair.

All Other Photographs: Page: x(b), xi(t), David Young-Wolff/PhotoEdit; xii, The Stock Market; xiv(l), Bob Daemmrich Photography; xiv(r), Myrleen Ferguson/PhotoEdit; xv(t), David Young-Wolff/PhotoEdit; xv(b), Comstock; xvi(r), David Young-Wolff/PhotoEdit.

UNIT A: Harcourt Brace & Company Photographs: Page: A4-A5, A6(t), A6(c), A6(b), Terry D. Sinclair; A8, A9, Weronica Ankarorn; A10-A11, Terry D. Sinclair; A14, Weronica Ankarorn; A15, A18, A20(t), A20(b), A21, A28, Terry D. Sinclair; A29(t), Weronica Ankarorn; A36, A38, A39, A40, A41, A42, A44-A45, Terry D. Sinclair; A44, Maria Paraskevas; A47, A49, A53, A54, A55, A60, A63, A66-A67, A73(bg), A73, Terry D. Sinclair; A75, Weronica Ankarorn; A77(t), A77(b), A82, A84, A90-A91(inset), A91(tr), A92(t), A92(b), Terry D. Sinclair; A93(t), Weronica Ankarorn.

All Other Photographs: Page: Divider Page A, Peter Menzel; A1, A2-A3, Tony Freeman/PhotoEdit; A3(inset), F.K. Smith; A7, Mike Morris/Unicorn Stock Photos; A12(border), Joyce Photographics/Photo Researchers; A12, Johnny Autery; A12(inset), M. Antman/The Image Works; A13, Jan Halaska/Photo Researchers; A14(inset), Bill Horsman/Stock, Boston; A16(t), M. Antman/The Image Works; A16(c), John Elk III/Stock, Boston; A16(bl), Jeff Greenberg/Unicorn Stock Photos; A16(r), Courtesy Thermometer Corp. of America/Color-Pic; A17(tl), David R. Frazier/The Stock Solution; A17(tr), The Granger Collection, New York; A17(b), Tom Pantages; A20-A21(bg), Craig Tuttle/The Stock Market; A23, Kent & Donna Dannen/Photo Researchers; A23 (inset), Bob Daemmrich/The Image Works; A25, Charles Krebs/The Stock Market; A26, E.R. Degginger/Color-Pic; A29(ct), Myrleen Ferguson Cate/PhotoEdit; A29(cb), Bob Daemmrich/Stock, Boston; A29(b), Kees Van Den Berg/Photo Researchers; A30, Myrleen Ferguson Cate/PhotoEdit; A30(inset), Richard Pasley/Stock, Boston; A31(l), Joyce Photographics/Photo Researchers; A31(r), E.R. Degginger/Color Pic; A32-A33, J.A. Borowczyk/The Stock Solution; A33, Tom McCarthy/Unicorn Stock Photos; A34(t), Lee Rentz/Bruce Coleman, Inc.; A34(c), A34(b), E.R. Degginger/Color-Pic; A35(tl), Nancy L. Simmerman/Bruce Coleman, Inc.; A35(tr), E.R. Degginger/Color-Pic; A35(b), Phil Degginger/Color-Pic; A42-A43(bg), E.R. Degginger/Color-Pic; A42-A43(inset), Tony Freeman/PhotoEdit; A46(border), Dan Sudia/Photo Researchers; A46, Timothy Schultz/Bruce Coleman, Inc.; A46(inset), Photri; A48, Phil Degginger/Color-Pic; A49(bg), H. Bluestein/Photo Researchers; A50-A51, Peter Menzel; A54-A55(bg), Tony Freeman/PhotoEdit; A56-A57, Nawrocki Stock Photo; A57, Ralf-Finn Hestoft/SABA; A58-A59, Susan Poa/Times Picayune/AP/Wide World Photos; A59(t), Howard B. Bluestein/Photo Researchers; A60(bg), E.R. Degginger/Color-Pic; A61(all), Howard B.

R30